Giles County
Tennessee

MISCELLANEOUS
WILLS

1830–1857

WPA RECORDS

Heritage Books
2024

HERITAGE BOOKS

AN IMPRINT OF HERITAGE BOOKS, INC.

Books, CDs, and more—Worldwide

For our listing of thousands of titles see our website
at
www.HeritageBooks.com

A Facsimile Reprint
Published 2024 by
HERITAGE BOOKS, INC.
Publishing Division
5810 Ruatan Street
Berwyn Heights, MD 20740

Nashville, Tennessee
The Historical Records Survey
April 23, 1940

International Standard Book Number
Paperbound: 978-0-7884-9070-5

The Historical Records Survey

Luther H. Evans, Director
Dan Lacy, Regional Supervisor
Madison Bratton, State Director
Penelope J. Allen, Supervisor

Division of Professional and Service Projects

Florence Kerr, Assistant Commissioner
Blanche M. Ralston, Chief Regional Supervisor
Betty Hunt Luck, State Director

WORK PROJECTS ADMINISTRATION

F. C. Harrington, Commissioner
Malcolm J. Miller, Regional Director
Harry S. Berry, State Administrator

WPA RECORDS

The WPA Records are, for the most part, carbon copies of the original that was typed on onion skin paper during the Depression. Since these records were typed on poor machines by people who did not type well either and read by persons not always sure of the older handwritten material, the results are often less that perfect.

We have made every attempt to make as good a copy as can be made from these older papers. Sometimes there are water stains and burned edges around the paper.. This is the results of a fire at the home of one of the workers, Mrs. Penelope Allen, who was over most of the project.

The WPA Records are now very scattered between the State Archives, various Public and Private Libraries and other collections. Some day, there is a hope that all of these can be collected and stored in one place. In spite of their many mistakes and problems, these are still the most complete collection of Tennessee records found anywhere.

GILES COUNTY

MISCELLANEOUS WILLS
1815-1860

TABLE OF CONTENTS

Parham, Ephriam, (1818) 84
Parker, Jeremiah, (1840) 85
Patrick, John Sr. (1827) 86
Paul, John, (1823) 87
Paxton, James M. (1818) 88
Petty, Mathias, (1832) 89
Porter, Reese, (1822) 90, 91
Pully, James, (1837) 92
Pyle, Sarah (1841) 93

Rainey, Sarah, (1842) 94
Reding, Stephen, (1830) 95
Reed, Samuel C. (1844) 96
Roberson, Christopher, (1830) 97
Roper, Denny, (1845) 98
Rowe, Joseph, (1845) 99

Shelton, Edmund, (1846) 100
Smith, Buckner, (1818) 101
Smith, John, (1818) 102
Smith, John W. (1837) 103
Stockton, Margaret, (1818) 104
Stone, Thomas C. (1844) 105

Tacker, Andrew E.Y. (1857) 106,107
Tacker, Joshua, (1848) 108
Taylor, George, (1842) 109
Thomson, David, (1831) 110
Trigg, William, (1839) 111
Tucker, George B. (1859) 112
Tucker, Will T. (1937) 113

U (None)

Vick, Jonas, (1840) 114

Wagstaff, John, (1858) 115
Wheeler, Benjamin, (1842) 116
Wheeler, Nancy, (1853) 117
Wilkins, Tabitha, (1817) 118
Williams, Margaret, (1854) 119
Williams, Thomas, (1849) 120

Yarbrough, Britton, (1815) 121
Yarbrough, David, (1841) 122,123
Young, John, (1837) 124,125
Young, Thomas, (1841) 126,127
Young, Thomas L. (1843) 128

ELISHA ABERNATHY

WILL 1857

July 28th. 1857. The last Will and Testament of Elisha Abernathy of Giles County, State of Tennessee.

I, Elisha Abernathy, being of sound mind and memory, do make and publish my last Will and Testament in manner and form following:
First, I give to my wife, Mary Abernathy all of my estate, consisting of land, negroes, horses, cattle, hogs, Sheep, Household and kitchen furniture & during her natural life and widowhood, and upon her decease, I will that the tract of land, on which I Now reside, remain for the benefit of my children by the said Mary Abernathy, until the youngest child becomes of age, the balance of my estate, I will that it be sold and all my just debts be paid, with burial & funeral expenses, of which the remainder shall be equally divided among my five children, towit: Richard, Claryann, Emily, Fredrick, Henry and Sarah.
Having divided my estate soon after my intermarriage with the said Mary Abernathy and give to my older children, by my first wife, as much or more than I will leave to my younger children, I will that the older children, by my first wife shall not have any of my estate now to be divided, having received their portion of my estate.
In witness whereof, I have hereto set my hand and seal, the twenty eighth day of July, one thousand, eight hundred and fifty seven.

ELISHA ABERNATHY (Seal)

Test John A. Grugett (Seal)
John H. Birdsong (Seal)

And I hereby appoint my faithful friend, John H. Birdsong, Administrator of my Will, in testimony whereof, I set my hand and seal & date above.

ELISHA ABERNATHY (Seal)

Test John A. Grugett (Seal)
John E. Tennery (Seal)

GILES COUNTY.

WM. ANDERSON

WILL 1825

In the name of God Amen.

I, William Anderson, of the County of Giles and State of Tennessee, being of perfect mind and memory, but knowing that it is appointed for all men once to die, and wishing not to die intestate, do make and ordain this my last Will and Testament, towit.

1st, I recomend my soul to the Almighty and request that my Executors hereinafter mentioned should bury my body in a decent & Chriatain manner.

2nd. As to the worldly goods to which it has pleased the Almighty to help me, I dispose of the same in the following manner, towit.

1st. to my daughter Peggy Howard and her husband Hiram Howard, I give one feather bed, one cow and calf, which articles I have heretofore delivered to them.

2nd. To my son John F. Anderson, I give one mare & saddle, one cow & calf, & fifteen head of hogs, which articles I have heretofore delivered to him.

3rd. To my daughter Martha Graham and her husband William Graham, I give one bed and cow and calf, which I heretofore delivered to them.

4th. To my daughter Betsy Anderson, I give one cow & calf, one feather bed & furniture to be delivered to her whenever she becomes of age or marries in my lifetime & deliver them, the are not to be delivered by my executors, whereinafter mentioned, but if she should become of age or marry in my lifetime then they are to be delivered th her by my said executors,

5th. To my wife, Martha, I give all the balance of my estate, after the payment of my just debts of whatsoever kind or description during her natural life, and after her death, All the personal Estate to be equally divided between my children, Peggy Howard, John F. Anderson, Martha Graham, Betsy Anderson and Sevier Anderson.

6th. I give and bequeath to my son, Sevier Anderson, after the death of his motherm the tract of land on which I now live, containing by estimation fifteen acres be the same more or less, to have and to hold to him, his heirs forever & to his only proper use, benefit and behalf, Also a horse, saddle, & bridle, a bed & bed clothes, & a cow and calf, to be delivered at my death, and he is to have an equal part in the balance of the Estate after the death of my wife.

7th. It is my Will and desire that my beloved wife, Martha and son Sevier, be Executor and Executrix to this my last Will and Testament, and that they proceed to execute the same by proving this my will without being required to give any security for their Executorship.

8th. I hereby revoke all other Wills by me heretofore made, and declair this to be my last will and testament.

In Testimony whereof, I have hereunto set my hand and seal this 8th January 1825.

           his
     WILLIAM X ANDERSON (Seal)
         mark

Signed, sealed & published in presence of,
Alfred M. Harris
Jeremiah Parker

BURTON BEASLEY

WILL 1817

In the name of God, Amen.

I, Burton Beasley of the County of Giles & State of Tennessee, being
in a low State of Health and apprehensive of departing this life in a
short time but as yet of a sound mind and perfect recollection doe make
this my last will and testament, viz;

I give to my beloved wife, Delylee Beasley, during her widowhood all my
property both real and personal & my will is that she my beloved wife keep
our children together & raise them & that nothing be sold but to satisfy
just debts & in that case she to direct what shall be sold, and should my
beloved wife marry again, then in that case my will is that she, my beloved
wife receive a childs part of the whole of my estate, both real and personal

Signed and sealed in presence of

James Duford &)
Moses Grisham)

    X

  his mark

This 28th day of November
1817.

     his
BURTON X BEASLEY
     mark

JACOB G. BRADEN

WILL 1857

I, Jacob G. Braden, make this my last Will and Testament, revoking all others by me made.

1st. My will is that all my just debts be paid with the first money that comes into the hands of my executors, after my death.

2nd. My will is that the Levi Hayn's tract of land and the uper end of my land that is known as the Catherine Puckett tract of land be sold so much thereof as shall pay my debts.

3rd. My will is, after my debts are paid that my wife, Susan Braden and Harriett Braden and my two youngest children be made equal with my second wife's children by the property made to them by their Grandfather, Mathew Johnson.

4th. After that is done there is to be an equal division between all my children of all that is left.

I appoint John Wilson Johnson, my Executor of this my last will, this 4th day of December, 1857.

Signed, sealed and acknowledged in presas of

L.W. Shields x

Joseph East x   Tests

This 4th day of December 1857

Jacob G. Braden   (Seal)

MARY CALVERT

WILL 1842

Know all men by these present that whereas I, Mary Calvert of Giles
County, State of Tennessee in and by my letter of Attorney, bearing date
did make, constitute and appoint my attorney for recovery of all debts and
sums of money whatsoever due to me the said Mary Calvert, from the estate
of John Hunt Dec. as by the said letter of attorney may appear, now know
ye that I the said Mary Calvert have revoked, countermanded, annulled and
made void, and by these present do revoke, countermand, annul and make
void the said letter of Attorney and all power and authority thereby given
to the said Andrew Calvert, and whereas I the said Mary Calvert, wishing
that what may yet be coming to me from the Estate above named be equally
divided between my daughters, Martha Wray, Polly Walker and Jane Davis &
my son Andrew Calvert do hereby constitute John Wray & Phillips Walker,
with the power of Attorney, or as the case may be my executors to settle
all my business hoping that it will be settled amiably, and I further bequeath unto my grand daughter, Mary A. Davis, my bed and bedding and now
by the presence, I do hereby constitute this my last will and testament
and furthermore declair that should there be any terms or techinical
phases missing or wrong used that no advantage is to be taken in law.
In witness thereof I have set my mark this 7th day of January A.D. 1842.

           her
      MARY x CALVERT (Seal)
         mark

Signed sealed and delivered in presence of
Jeremiah McConnell, Jurat
Josiah N. Lawrence, Jurat

JAMES COLDWELL

WILL 1844

I, James Coldwell, Senior, considering the uncertainity of this mortal
life and being of sound mind and memory, blessed be Almighty God for the
same, do hereby make this my last will and testament, herebyrevoking all
former wills by me made, In manner and form following towit,
First, I give and bequeath unto my beloved wife Sally Coldwell, the tract
of land on which I now reside, all the preishable property of which I am
now in possession, and so many slaves towit, namely: Houston, Molly,
Sally & Daniel, during her natural life, and after my said wife's death
it is my will that said slaves be equally divided among my children, with
the exception of Alexander Coldwell & Grandville Coldwell, to whom it is
my will that they just have one hundred dollars each out of all my property and no more either real or personal, monied or perishable.
Secondly, I give and bequeath unto my son Robert Coldwell, the tract of
land that I purchased at the sale of John Snipes decd. on which my son,
Jackson Coldwell now resides to said Robert & his heirs forever. All the
balance of the slaves to be equally divided among my following named
children, towit: Margaret Tucker, Susan Campbell, Mary Daugherty,
Elizabeth Tucker, Robert Coldwell, Jefferson & Jackson Coldwell & the heirs
of James Coldwell Jr. the said James Coldwell's children to have a joint
proportion equal to one of the just mentioned legatees.
Furthermore it is my will that all my just debts be paid.
It is my will that my son Claibourn Coldwell share equally with my named
children, Margaret Tucker, Susan Campbell, Mary Daugherty, Elizabeth
Tucker, Robert Coldwell, Jefferson Coldwell, & Jackson Coldwell, in my
former mentioned property.
And I hereby appoint my son, Robert Coldwell and my son in law Joab
Campbell, Executor's to this my last will and testament hereby revoking
all others by me made heretofore,
In witness whereof I the said James Coldwell, Senior do hereunto set my
hand and affix my seal this the 8th day of January one thousand eight
hundred and forty four.

Attests   JAMES COLDWELL (Seal)
D.J. Moore, Jurat
H.S. Goldsberry, Jurat

ROSWELL COLLINS

WILL 1837

We, Francis Fergerson and Richard G. Tucker, do state that the noncupative will of Roswell Collins was made by him on the 25th of October 1837. In our presence to which we were especially requested to bear witness by the testator himself in the presence of each other that it was made in his last sickness at his own dwelling and the same is as follows, towit, that his effects should be disposed of in the following manner after his decease.

First, That his beloved wife, Verlinda Jane Collins, should have the intire control of all of his property without controll or accountability after paying off all his just debts and secondly, that his wife should have the guardianship of his children.

Made out and signed by us November 31st 1839.

Francis Fergerson &
Richard G. Tucker

LEWIS CONNER

WILL 1843

In the name of God, Amen.

I, Lewis Conner of Giles County, Tennessee, being quite weak in body, but of sound mind and memory, do make my last will and testament in the following manner, that is to say, after payment of my debts, which are few and small, I will and direct that my Executors hereinafter named, shall keep my Estate together and carry on my system of business as heretofore at my different farms, my tan yard to be discontinued, but all the tan yard furniture, apparatus and fixtures to be retained and not sold, until my son, James shall be sufficeintly experienced, for him and my Executors to deside upon, the propriety of his renewing the tanning business, in which event I will and direct that he be permitted by my executors to do so, and that he have for that purpose the use of said tan yard and fixtures.

I will and direct that when either or any of my children arrive at the age of twenty years that my Executors give off to them their full distributive portion of my Estate, and the remaining portion of my Estate still be kept together after each successive division, as my children arrive at twenty years as aforesaid, untill the youngest shall attain to that age.

I will my riding carriage, carriage horses and my servant Peyton, the driver to my beloved wife, Nancy A. Conner, over and above an equal distributive share of my other Estate with my children, and she is hereby left at liberty to continue her said distributive portion of my said Estate in common, to be kept together with the balance, or separated from the balance of my Estate and be held by her in severalty, as she may prefer, and at any time she may direct and require.

I will and direct that what money I have on hand at my death shall by my Executor be kept at interest in good solvent hands, and well secured, to be disposed of as the balance of my Estate, and in the same manner equally amongst my wife and children.

It is my will that all my children remain with my wife and be supported and educated annually out of the joint & common Estate until they receive perportions of my said estate, or volentarily leave the paternal roof and home.

Whenever Lydia Lewis, the wife of Fielding Lewis, or any other person for her shall tender to my Executors or either of them, the amount of money which I Paid for a negro man named Stephen, recently sold under a deed of trust as the property of the said Fielding Lewis, and lawful interest thereon to the time of payment, I will and direct that my said Executors shall convey said slave Stephen to the said Lydia Lewis, and her children for their sole use and benefit, separate from the said Fielding Lewis.

I constitute and appoint my wife Nancy A. Conner, my brother William Conner and my brother in law, William W. Patton, Executors to execute this my last and only will. In witness whereof I have hereunto set my hand and seal this 3rd day of June, A.D. 1843

                                        LEWIS CONNER (Seal)

Signed and published in presence of us,
E.D. Jones, Jurat
Samuel Y. Anderson, Jurat

JOHN C. COURTNEY

WILL 1838

State of Tennessee, Giles County.

I, John C. Courtney of the State & County aforesaid, being of sound mind and memory, do make this my last will and Testament hereby revoking all others.

Item: I give and bequeath all my Estate real and personal to David H. Abernathy.

Item: I appoint David H. Abernathy, my Executor of this my last will and testament.

In testimony whereof I have hereunto set my hand and seal this the twenty sixth day of December in the year of our Lord one thousand eight hundred thirty eight.

John C. Courtney, (Seal)

Witness
Joseph Goode, Jurat
Thomas Botts, Jurat
P.W. Phelps

ARCHIBALD CROCKETT

WILL 1839

In the Name of God, Amen.

I, Archibald Crockett, of the County of Giles and State of Tennessee, considering the uncertainity of this mortal life and being of sound and perfect mind and memory, blessed be to God for the same, do make and publish this my last will and testament in manner and form following:

First, I give and bequeath unto my beloved wife, Elizabeth Crockett, all that part of my land that I now live on, beginning at John Cochran's southwest corner on a beach then running south to Robinson's fork of Richland Creek, thence up said creek as it meanders to the mouth of the branch above my spring, thence up said branch as it meanders to my North boundary line, thence with the said line west to the beginning.

I also give and bequeath to my daughter, Dovy P. Cochran, and the heirs of her body, the place where she now lives on, beginning at Hugh Kerr's south west corner, a elm, thence running north with Kerr's line to Robison fork, thence down said Creek as it meanders to where James Montgomery's line crosses said creek, thence south with said creek, thence with said line to whites line, thence east with said line to the beginning.

I also give and bequeath to my daughter Violet P. Millican and the heirs of her body forever that part of my land whereon she now lives, beginning at a large poplar, my north east corner, running west as far as to include all Millicans farm by a line running south to my south boundary line, thence east to Armours corner, thence north to place of beginning.

I also give and bequeath to my son Robert C. Crockett, that part of my land where Robert C. Armor, now lives, beginning at John Cochran south west corner, a beach running south forty five poles then west to Montgomery's line, thence north to Montgomery's corner, thence west to my south west corner, a beach thence north to Lane's south west corner, thence east to the beginning.

I also give and bequeath to my daughter, Jane A. McKnight, that part of my land where M. Dickey now lives to be hers and the heirs of her body forever beginning at Robinson's fork where my line and Montgomery's crosses the creek running north to his and my corner, thence south to Robert C. Crockett's corner, thence east to his south east corner, thence south to Robinson fork, thence down the creek as it meanders to the place of beginning.

I also give and bequeath to my son David G. Crockett, that part of my land where A. Freeman now lives, beginning at John Montgomerys south west corner running south to Robinson fork, thence up the creek to my corner of a tract of land, I bought from G.W. Camble, thence south to my corner in Rivers line thence east with my line to Violet P. Millicans corner, thence north with her line to her north west corner thence west to the beginning.

I also give and bequeath to my daughter Elizabeth J. Crockett a part of my land beginning at the mouth of a branch above my spring running up the branch as it meanders to my north boundary line, thence east to John Montgomery's south west corner, thence to Robinson fork, thence down the creek as it meanders to the beginning to be hers and the heirs of her body, if any, forever.

I also give my tract of land lying on the ridge to my two daughters,

Dovy F. Cochran and Elizabeth Crockett, to be equally divided between them.
I also give to my beloved wife Elizabeth Crockett, my old black mare named
Antrim, and also my oxen and wagon, and one mare colt, roan and one old
horse named Tom.
I also give to my daughter, Elizabeth Crockett, one young horse called
Buck, and one cow and calf and one bed and furniture.
I give to my daughter, Violet F. Millican, one young mare colt called
Gaggy and all the rest of my goods and chattels, of whatsoever kind I
give to my wife Elizabeth.

State of Tennessee, Giles County, February 2nd. 1839
To the Worshipfull County Court of Giles:
It is my desire that David G. Crockett should be appointed Executor of my
husbands will, to pay the debts and protect what is due, as the same will
be done out of my own purse, without his giving any bond or security &.

                                        ELIZABETH CROCKETT

Test
Wm M. Kerr

ROBERT CROCKETT

WILL 1824

In the Name of God, Amen.

I, Robert Crockett, of the State of Tennessee & County of Giles, considering the uncertainity of this mortal life, and being of sound and perfect mind and memory, belssed be to God for the same, do make and publish this my last Will and Testament in manner and form following (that is to say) First, I give and bequeath unto my two daughters, Derius & Rachel, my negro girl Sarah, her & her offspring, if any belong equally to them both, my bead & furniture and the seventy five dollar note I hold on Jacob Cochran my son in law due the 25th day of December 1826.
I give and bequeath to my daughter, Rachel, I willfurther that my riding chair and all the goods and chattels of every kind belonging to me, be sold on a credit of twelve months, and the money equally divided amongst my five oldest daughters, and the other note I hold on Jacob Cochran, of twenty five dollars to be divided as above amongst my said five oldest daughters, after all my just debts are paid and I will that such of my books as is marked with the name of Archabald Crockett be given to him, and all that are marked with the name of either of my six daughters be given to them, and I will that my son, A. Crockett & my son in law James Davill be the Executors of this my last and Testament, and I do hereby revoke all former wills by me made, in testimony whereof, I have hereunto set my hand & seal this twenty second day of June eighteen hundred & twenty four in presence of witnesses.

ROBERT CROCKETT (Seal)

James Cochran, Jurat
Wm. Cochran, Jurat

WILLIAM C. FLOURNOY

WILL 1838

I, William C. Flournoy of the County of Giles and State of Tennessee being in low state of health but of sound mind do make and publish this my last will and testament as follows: I give and desire my whole estate real and personal and mixed to my wife, Martha Flournoy, for and during her natural life or widowhood to have the free use and enjoyments of the rents and profits of my land, negroes & other estate during said periods, out of which however, she is to raise, support and educate my children in such way as she deems most proper. If my wife should marry, my will and desire is that she shall have one third of my whole estate, real, personal, the other two thirds of my estate to be equally divided amongst my children. If my wife should not marry, then at her death I wish the whole of my estate to be equally divided among my children, my will and desire is, that if my wife should think proper to do so, she may sell the house and lots whereon I now live in the town of Pulaski at such price as she deems best and apply proceeds in payment of the tract of land, which I lately purchased of Peter Swanson, also if my wife should not think it proper to do this, my will and desire is that she have power to rescind the purchase so made of said Swanson,

I hereby appoint my wife Executrix of this my last will and testament, My will and desire is that she also act as the guardian of my children until they are twenty one years of age, and that she shall be allowed to quallify both as Executrix of my will and guardian of my children without giving any security for performing the duties that belong to said office.

In witness whereof I have set my hand and seal this the 13th day of September 1838.

WILL C. FLOURNOY (Seal)

Signed, sealed & executed)
in presence of
D.M. Field, Jurat
Silas Flournoy, Jurat
A. Wright, Jurat

JAMES FORD

WILL 1840

By the Will of God, Amen.

I, James Ford, being possessed of my right mind, do make and publish this as my last will & testament, hereby revoking and making void all other wills by me at any time made.

First, I direct that my funeral expenses and all my debts be paid as soon after my death as possible, out of any money that I may die possessed of or may first come into the hands of my Executor.

2nd. I give and bequeath to my wife, Nancy Ford, my tract of land on which I now live, with all things appertaining thereto, during her life-time and at her death to be sold to the highest bidder & the money re-ceived therefrom to equally divided between my children, Polly Kerr, the heirs of Lucy Garner, John Ford, Nancy Ramsey, James S. Ford, Andrew E. Ford & Bartlett S. Ford. Thereby I give and bequeath to my sons, Andrew E. Ford & Bartlett S. Ford each, one cow and calf and one bed and furniture. My will further is that my Executor sell all my stock of horses, hogs, cows and sheep, and my household & kitchen furniture, together with my corn, fodder and farming utensils (except so much as my wife Nancy wishes to retain for her benefit) to the highest bidder & divide the proceeds amongst my children as above named. Likewise I will that my Executor hire out my boy Frank during my wife, Nancy Fords life time. At her death to be sold & the money divided equally amongst my children. I further request that my son, James S. Ford, take possession of my land and use it as he may think best during my wife, Nancy Fords lifetime, provided he shall take good care of her during that time and give her any necessary she may require. I do nominate and appoint James S. Ford, my executor in witness whereby I have set my hand and seal this 10th day of December 1840.

JAMES FORD (Seal)

Signed, sealed and published in our presence and we have suscribed our names in the presence of the Testators, this day and date above written.

Thomas A. Westmoreland, Jurat
Vachel Davis, Jurat

P. GARLAND

WILL. 1817

God have mercy on me and in his name I make and ordain this my last Will and Testament, revoking all others.

I will one third part of all my estate to my dear wife and give her all my household and kitchen furniture during her material life & then to be divided between her two daughters, Juliana & Maria Luisa. The balance of my estate I wish equally divided between these before mentioned two children and Mrs. Alexanders children from Bonaparth Jefferson, to Worter Waller, all to have equal proportions, Amen.

P. GARLAND

9th Oct. 1817
Acknowledged by him this 9th Oct. 1817

The shortness of time and scarcety of paper is the cause of this short will.

Proven Nov. 1818.

AGATHA GARRETT

WILL 1830

In the Name of God, Amen.

I, Aggatha Garrett, of the County of Giles and State of Tennessee being weak in body but of sound mind and memory, considering the uncertainity of this mortal life, do make and publish this my last will and Testament in the manner and form following:

For and in the consideration of the affection and kindness of my son, Milton, and in consideration of a just claim he has on me as his guardian, of about fifty five dollars and interest from the time he came of age, do (after a decent burial and a discharge of all the just claims against me) will and bequeath to my said son, Milton Garrett, the tract of land on which I now live consisting by computation of about twenty acres, together with all my household and kitchen furniture and whatever else to me of right belonging, and I do farther request that after my decease the said Milton be made and lawfully constituted the Executor of this my last will and Testament.

In testimony hereof, I have hereunto set my hand and offered my seal this 25th day of November 1830.

her

AGGATHA X GARRETT (Seal)

mark

James Moores
John W. Darnett

WINSTON C. GATLIN

WILL   1844

In the name of God Amen.

I, Winston C. Gatlin of the County of Giles, State of Tennessee, being weak in body but of sound and disposing mind and memory, and being impressed with the uncertainity of life and knowing the certainity of death, I make and ordain this my last will and testament in manner and form following, To wit.

Item 1st.. My will and desire is that my necessary funeral expenses be paid first out of my estate and secondly I wish all my just debts paid.

Item 2nd. After all my just debts are paid I give to my beloved wife Nancy Gatlin, all the balance of my property of every description during her natural life, to be managed by her as she may think best for the support and education of my children and my wish is for my said wife to give off to my children as they may become of age or marry, such portions of my estate as she can spare, charging each child with such portions given off in order that each one may have an equal interest in my estate.

Item 3rd. At the death of my said wife, my will and desire is that whatever may be remaining in her hands, of my Estate, I wish equally divided amongst my living children.

Item 4th. My will and desire is that my Executor hereafter to be named dispose of such of my property as may seem best for the interest of my Estate may require and lastly, I hereby appoint my wife, Nancy Gatlin Executrix to this my last will and testament, given under my hand and seal this 12th day of December 1844.

WINSTON C. GATLIN (Seal)

Signed , sealed and
acknowledged in the
presence of
Wm. D. Abernathy, Jurat
Matthew Davenport, Jurat

GEORGE GIBSON

WILL 1835

I, George Gibson, of the County of Giles and State of Tennessee, farmer, do make and publish this my last will & testament, hereby revoking and making void all former will by me at any time heretofore made, And first I direct that after my decease, my body be decently intered wherever my beloved wife, Ann, may think proper to place it, and to such worldly Estate as it has pleased God to intrust me with, I dispose of the same as follows:

First, I direct that all my debts, and funeral expenses be paid as soon after my decease as possible, out of the first monies that shall come into the hands of my Executor from any portion of my Estate.

I also hereby will and bequeth to my beloved daughter Jane, one sorrel mear, saddle & Bridle, two cows, one cupboard, one beaure, the balance of all my property, rights and possessions I give and bequeth to my beloved wife, Ann, for her sustainance and support, during her life, and I do hereby make and ordain my beloved son, Joseph, my executor of this, my last will and testament.

In witness whereof I, George Gibson, the testator have to this my will written on one sheet of paper, set my hand and seal this 4th day of March 1835.

GEORGE GIBSON (Seal)

Signed, sealed and delivered in the presence of each other.
J.J. Dickey
Thomas Rea
Benjamin Allen

JOHN GORDON .

WILL 1834

In the Name of God, Amen.

I, John Gordon of Giles County and State of Tennessee, being of sound
and disposing mind and perfect memory, blessed be Allmighty God for the
same, I do make and publish this my last will & testament, revoking all
others, heretofore made by me.

First, I give and bequeath unto my wife, Elizabeth Gordon, all of my
land, during her widowhood, and if she marries, I dispose of it in the
following manner, towit:

I give the whole of my land to my son James M. Gordon, at my widow's
death, the land to be James M. Gordon's. I also give to my wife Elizabeth
the following negroes herein named, John, Kale, Tinoe, Alfred, Dilly &
Harriett, and if she marries, the said negroes to be disposed of in the
following manner, towit: They are to be equally divided among all of my
children except Catharine M. Alexander and Elizabeth McCanless. I also give
my wife, one bed and furniture forever.

I also give and bequeath unto my two grandchildren, Lamer M. McCanless
and Casa McCanless, a negro boy named Wat, to be equally divided between
the said children, and that is their full portion of my estate.

I also give to my two grandchildren, Morgan L. Alexander & John
Allexander a negro girl named Pat, to be equally divided between said
children, and that is their full share of my estate.

I also give and bequeath unto my son John P.W.P. Gordon, one bed and
furniture.

I also give my daughter, Rebecca D. Gordon, one negro girl named
Elizabeth, one bed and furniture, one cow and calf.

I also give to my son, James M. Gordon, one negro man names Charles,
and one dark bay horse, one bed and furniture, all of perishable property
to be sold by my Executor except what I have heretofore willed away, and
if there is not enough to pay my just debts, the negro girl named Harriett,
that I willed my wife is to be sold by my executor for to satisfy the same
and if there is any money left, it is to be divided equally between all of
my living children, but all of my just debts to be paid before any division
of my estate. The negro girl named Manda, which my daughter Casa McCanless
has in her possession, is to remain hers forever.

I also give my four daughters hereafter named towit, Casa McCanless,
Mary McCanless, Hannah Alexander and Massey Parsons, the sum of five dollars
each. I also nominate and appoint Harrington L. Field, my executor to this
my last will. February 15th 1834.

JOHN GORDON (Seal)

Test. Henry T. Butler
Test. Hiriam Anderson

JOHN GRACY

WILL 1838

State of Tennessee, Giles County
November 1st. 1838

I, John Gracy, do make this my last will and testament of my concent, would and without amiss.

First, I will that after my death, that so much of my surplus property be sold as will pay my just debts.

Second, I will to my beloved wife, Rachel Gracy, all my household and kitchen furniture, or if she should die first the one half thereof to my daughter, Arixana L. Gracy, and the other half to be sold and my administrators reserve and pay over said money with all other money's that I may leave to the heirs of Cynthia Davidson as they come of age.

Third, I will to my four oldest children, say Sewel Gracy, John Gracy, Jane L. Stewart and Mary Calhoons, $5.00.

Fourth, I will to my son, W.S.B. Gracy, a clear right of a horse he owes me for.

Fifth, I will to my son, J.B. Gracy, my blacksmith tools.

Sixth, I will to my youngest daughter, A.L. Gracy, a horse, bridle and saddle, with a good bed and bed stead and furniture.

Seventh, I will to my daughter, Cynthia Davidson, two beds and steds and a bureau.

Eighth, I will to my youngest son, F.J.R. Gracy, my farming tools, and on condition that he stays with and takes care of us, his parents and his sister, A.L. Gracy. He is to have all my land, but is not to have possession of the building without consent. But if he should marry and think proper to make a settlement on the land after supporting the family he is to have all he can make over, but shall not be at liberty to sell the land without the concent of his mother and sister A.L. Gracy, and all sails by him shall be null and void without concent.

Ninth, If said F.J.R. Gracy, should prefer not staying and taking care of his mother and sister, the home shall be the property of my beloved wife.

Tenth, All the stock not sold to pay my debts are to remain on the farm for the support of the family.

This day and date above named (N.B.) If my beloved wife, Rachel Gracy should die before me. and my land be rate, that part coming to Cynthia Davidson, is to go to her lawful heirs, and it to be paid as above directed.

JOHN GRACY (Seal)

W.N. Gracy &
J.B. Gracy, Admrs.

Test.
James Paisley, Jurat
James D. Paisley, Jurat

WILLIAM H.R. GRACY

WILL 1864

March 16, 1864.

I, William H.R. Gracy, do make and publish this my last will and Testament, hereby revoking and making void all the wills by me at any time made.

First, I direct that my funeral expenses and all my debts, be paid out of the money that I may die possessed of, or the first money that may come into the hands of my Executors.

2nd. I give and bequeath to my beloved wife, Nancy S. Gracy, five negroes, towit: Nelly, Lancaser, Hetty, Letty and Claibourne.

3rd. I give and bequeath to my daughter, Elizabeth Ann Smith and her bodily heirs, one negro girl named Sally, one horse and bridle & saddle, one bed, bedsted and furniture.

4th. I give and bequeath to my daughter, Adaline B. Gracy, when she arrives at the age of twenty one, and her bodily heirs, one negro girl named Janie, one horse, saddle & Bridle, one bed, bedsted and furniture,

5th. I give and bequeath to my son John S. Gracy, and his heirs, one negro boy named Andy, one horse, saddle & bridle, one bed, bedsted & furniture.

6th. I give and bequeath to my daughter Mariah F. Gracy at the age of twenty one, and her bodily heirs, one negro girl named Mary, one horse saddle & bridle, one bed bedsted, & furniture,

7th. I give and bequeath to my daughter? Tranquilla R. Gracy, & her bodily heirs, at the age of twenty one, one negro girl named Martha, one horse, saddle & bridle, one bed, bedsted & furniture.

8th. I give and bequeath to my daughter Emarry B. Gracy, and her bodily heirs, when she arrives at the age of twenty one, one negro girl named Diza, one horse, one saddle & bridle, one bed, bedsted & furniture.

9th. I give and bequeath to my son, William C. Gracy, and his heirs at the age of twenty one, one negro boy named Fortune, one horse, saddle, & bridle, one bed, bedsted & furniture.

10th. I direct, that if any of the above named negroes, dies, except Elizabeth A. Smith's, I want the loss made equal up to the heir to which it belongs, out of the balance of my estate.

11th. I direct that my youngest heirs from Francis down, be made eaqual in their education with the oldest heirs out of the proceeds of my estate.

12th. I direct that all of my perishable property be sold except so much as will do my family to support on.

13th. I give and bequeath to my beloved wife, Nancy S. Gracy, my land on which I now live, and all other lands which belongs to me be hers to raise the family on as long as she lives or untill the youngest child becomes of age, then I want the land sold and the proceeds equally divided among all of heirs.

Lastly, I do hereby nominate and appoint Joseph B. Gracy & John W. Smith, my executors. In witness whereof I do, to this my last will, and set my hand and seal this 25th day February, 1854.

W.H.R. Gracy (Seal)

Signed in the presents of us and we suscribed our names in the presents of Testators the day and date above written.
David M. Waters &
James White, Jurat

ELVIN ERSKIN HARNEY

WILL 1851

I, Elvin Erskin Harney, of the County of Giles and State of Tennessee, do make and publish this my last will and testament as follows;

Item 1st. I will that all my just debts be paid out of the first money that may come into the hands of my executor from any portion of my estate.

Item 2nd. It is my will that five hundred dollars out of my estate be expended for enclosing and improving the burial grounds wher rests the remains of my beloved parents.

Item 3rd. I give and bequeath to my uncle James M. Harney, one thousand dollars.

Item 4th. The balance of my estate both real and personal I give and bequeath to my beloved brother, A.L. Harney, if he shall be living at the time of my decease, but if he should not survive me, then it is my will that all of my Estate both real and personal except the two first items in this will be given absolutely to my uncle Jas. M. Harney.

And I do hereby make and ordain my brother, A.L. Harney, Executor, to this my last will and testament.

In testimony whereof, I hereunto set my hand and affix my seal, this 14th day of October in the year of Our Lord, eighteen hundred and fifty one.

ELVIN ERSKIN HARNEY (Seal)

Tests.
Wm. F. Benson
Wm. L. Elerson

ROBERT S. HARRIS

WILL 1847

In the Name of God, Amen.

I, Robert S. Harris, being extreamly low and knowing that death is certain do make, ordain and appoint this my last will and testament.

First of all I want, I want my just debts paid by executor, out of the first money that comes to hand. I dont want any public sale of any of my farming tools, stock or property whatever.

My Executors are to have full power to sell any property that I am possessed of, if necessary, except my land and premises, that I wish my wife Mary P. Harris to remain in possession of. After my youngest son becomes of age, if they all agree to sell, and my wife Mary consents, they are then at liberty to sell.

I want some one of my sons to remain in the family for the protection of their mother & sisters, cultivate the land and make all they can to be enjoyed in common together, except my son who attends to the business, he must have a moderate pay for his services.As long as my two daughters remain with my wife and render common family servis, they are to be free from all charges.

I wish my wife to remain in possession of our little family of slaves, mother and all.

I make a special reserve of the boy Joe, that he is not to be sold untill my wife's death at any price.

As my heirs become of age and marry or leave their mother, I want them to have a good strong saddle horse, saddle & briddle, and whatever else my wife or Executor thinks can be spared with convenience. If they can't make enough from the farms, for the purposes I have expressed then I would be glad if they can buy or sell off one of them and make distribution of one of the young negroes. I would much rather, I dont want them sold out of the family.

I want my wife to remain in full possession of the house and household furniture of every description, during her life, as her children leave her help them to such things as she can spare, and they need.

At my wife's death, then I wish a general division of the young negroes. If they cant do that, sell one another, then they must sell to some good merciful man, for as much as they can get. I want my youngest son, Christopher, W. Harris to be sent to school untill he can read & write & calculate well. I want him to have my rifle gun, with positive injunction never to sell it. This was a dieing pledge to me, except that I want all my children to be made as equal as posable. If my wife, Mary should choose to marry, then she is to have what the law provides for widows.

Now I do appoint my Two sons, Nathan W. Harris & Robert Simpson Harris Executors to this my last will and testament, and they are not to be required to give any security. In testimony whereof, I the said Robert S. Harris, do hereunto put my hand and seal this 3rd day of July 1847.

ROBERT S. HARRIS (Seal)

Tests
Jesse Wells, Jurat
James B. Wells, Jurat

HARRISON D. HART

WILLS 1854

State of Tennessee & County of Giles.

I, Harrison D. Hart, do make and publish this as my last Will and Testament, hereby revoking and making void all other wills by me at any time made.

First, I direct my funeral expences and all my debts be paid as soon after my death as possible, out of any money I may die possessed of, or may first come into the hands of my Executor.

Secondly, I give and bequeath unto my beloved wife, all the lands I own, so long as she remains my widow. In the event she becomes the wife of another, I direct she remain on the land provided she mantain the children and cultivate and keep up the farm, right, untill the youngest child becomes eighteen years of age, then the land be sold on a one & two year credit and that she have three hundred dollars out of the proceeds of the land, and the remainder be equally divided between my heirs.

Lastly, I do hereby nominate and appoint Caleb Hart, my Executer. In witness whereof, O do to this my will, set my hand and seal this the 17th day of June 1854.

                                        HARRISON D. HART (Seal)

      Signed, sealed and published in our presence and we have subscribed our names in the presence of the Testator, this the 17th. day of June 1854.

James N. Paisley, Jurat
Calloway H. Tidwell, Jurat

ABSOLOM HARWELL.

WILLS 1818

In the name of God, Amen.

I, Absolom Harwell of the County of Giles and State of Tennessee, being in a low state of health but of perfect sense and memory, and knowing that it is appointed for all men once to die, do make and publish and ordain this my last will and testament in the manner and form following, that is to say, I lend to my beloved wife Rebecca Harwell, all my estate, both real and personal, consisting of one hundred acres of land, and seven negro slaves, towit: Phill, Manuel, Billy, Jenny, Jesse, Judeth & Lucky and their increases, my stock of all kinds, household and kitchen furniture, and plantations, utensils, to be enjoyed by her, my said wife Rebecca Harwell, during her widowhood, and at her marriage or decease, my desire is that the aforesaid negroes to wit, Phill, Manuel, Billy, Jenny, Jesse, and Judeth & Lucky & their increases, be equally divided by five men appointed by my executors, among my children towit, Hartwell Harwell, Henry Harwell, Martha Abernathy Harwell, Clayton Abernathy Harwell and Clara Ann Harwell, and if negroes cannot be equally divided among my said children then my desire is that the portions under value be made equal by money arising from the sale of such property as I shall hereafter appoint to be sold, And I further will and desire that that is any of my said children die before they marry the property descending to them, be equally divided among my surviving children, and I likewise further desire that mt said wife, Rebecca Harwell keep all my aforesaid children with her till they marry or arrive at the age of twenty one years, and give them such education as may be convenient for her. And I do also desire that the residue of my estate at the marriage or death of my said wife, Rebecca Harwell, be sold and the money arising from the sale thereof, save only a suffiency to equalise the lots in which the negroes may be divided be equal among my said children, and finally, I desire that mt wife, Rebecca Harwell, and Alan Abernathy be executors of this, my last will & Testament.

Given under my hand and seal this seventh day of January, one thousand eight hundred & eighteen.

ABSOLOM HARWELL (Seal)

Signed and acknowledged in presence of
Charles C. Abernathy, Jurat
Henry Scales, Jurat
Benjamin M. Schoggins, Jurat

A Codicil to the aforesaid will.
Be it known to all men by these presents, that, I Absolom Harwell, of the County of Giles and State of Tennessee, have made and declared my last will and testament in writing, bearing date the seventh day of January, one thousand eight hundred and eighteen. I the said Absolom Harwell, by this present Codicil do ratify and confirm my said last will and testament, and further desire that the executors of this my last will and testament having power to sell or not to sell the slaves, Manuel mentioned in my will and that the money gotten for him be added to my estate in a manner they may deem right, and my will is that this codicil be a part of my last will & testament and that the same be performed as if it had been written in

my will.

ABSOLOM HARWELL (Seal)

Signed in the presence of
Benj. Williams, Jurat
26th of April 1818

COLEMAN HARWELL

WILL. 1841

In the name of God, Amen.

I, Coleman Harwell, being of sound and perfect mind & memory, do make and publish this my last will and testament.

1st, I will that my executors to pay all my debts. In doing which I wish them to sell the lot of land on which my son Ambrose now lives.

2nd. I give and bequeath to my beloved wife, Catharine, my negro man, Jesse & Peggy his wife, my negor man Henry and my woman, Violett & her daughter, Mary & my big boy, Joe, during her life & at her death to be divided equally between my sons, Ambrose, Thomas & William.

3rd. I give and bequeath to my son Ambrose, my negro woman Candis & her two children, my boys, Miles and my girl, Sarah.

4th. I give and bequeath to my son Thomas, my boys, Jack & Willis & my girl Lucy.

5th. I give and bequeath to my son William, my boys, Sam and Hugh & my girl Martha.

My will further is, that the residue of my tract of land be divided into three equal parts, between my sons, Ambrose, Thomas & William. I further will that my beloved wife, Catharine live at my residence with one of my sons, which shall get that part of the land that contains the sd. residence at the death of my mother. I desire that my portion of her estate be equally divided between my sons as above named.

Lastly, as to the rest or remainder of my property, I wish it to be sold at the discretion of my Executors. I hereby appoint my sons, Ambrose, B. Harwell & William M. Harwell, Executors to this my last will & testament & do hereby release them from giving security & likewise revoke & make void all former wills by me ever made.

In testimony whereof, I do hereby set my hand & affix my seal this 11th. day of January 1841.

COLEMAN HARWELL (Seal)

Signed, sealed and published
in the presence of
C.L.M. Matlock
R.S. Harris
Jones A. King

FEATHERSTON HARWELL.

WILL 1843

My last Will and Testament, after my body is desantly burried in the Name of God, Amen.

I do will and bequeath my property as follows, viz: that my son, Buckner have two hundred dollars or thereabout the proceeds of the farm of next year, of cotton or otherwise as it is due him.

Item 2nd. That my daughter Sarah Ann, have two hundred dollars or thereabout as is recorded in the Clerk's Office, intended to come of the proceeds of the farm as soon as it can be had.

Item 3rd. That my daughter, Lamentine, have two hundred dollars or thereabout as is recorded in the Clerk's Office in Pulaski, to be raised from the proceeds of the farms as soon as it can be had.

Item 4th. That my negroes and family, remain together on the farm till my children is raised or becomes of age.

Item 5th. That my beloved wife, Eliza, have a child's part of land, negroes and everything belonging to my estate.

Item 6th. As my children marry they shall have a horse, saddle, & bridle, and bed.

Item 7th. When my youngest child becomes of age, I wish all my household & kitchen furniture & stock & tolls of every description sold and equally divided between my wife and children, allowing my daughter, Sarah Ann, one hundred dollars in addition to what I have already willed her.

Item 8th. Notwithstanding all that has been said, I have two negroes, Vis; George and Mason, if they shall conduct themselves well, untill my youngest child becomes of age, my will is that they shall be freed.

Item 9th. It is further understood, my sister Elizabeth Croos' son has a small interest in the tract of land on which I live, and that when the said son becomes of age that the said interest be perchased of him, and added to the balance of the tract, if it can be.

I further request that Lewis B. Marks, be my Executor. In testimony whereof, I have hereunto set my hands and seal this twenty six day of November 1843.

F. Harwell (Seal)

Teste.
Wm. Harwell, Jurat
H. Harwell, Jurat

GARDNER M. HARWELL.

WILL 1856

In the Name of God, Amen.

This 20th day of March in the year of our Lord 1856, I, Gardner M. Harwell of the State of Tennessee and County of Giles, being sick and weak in body but of perfect and sound mind and memory, and calling to mind the mortality of my body and knowing that it is appointed for all to die, do make and ordain this my last will and Testament, that is to say principally and first of all, I give and recommend my soul into the hands of God that gave it, and for my body I recommend it to the earth to be burried in a Christain like manner, and as touching such worldly estate, wherewith it hath pleased God to give me in this I give and dispose of the same in the manner and form following.

I give and bequeath to my daughter, Mary Tayler Huff, and my son in law William B. Huff, my plantation where I now live, with all the bildings and machinery, that is now upon it, except seven hundred and twelve dollars that the land I consider to be worth more than my negro property, I mean one share of my negro property, this seven hundred and twelve dollars, my will is that my son in law Willaim B. Huff keep that money in his hands by giving bond and security at six per cent, to pay it over to the two youngest children as they become of age or marry, my will is that this money is to be equally divided between my two youngest children when the first of them becomes of age ot marries. The oldest, I give her name, which is Madora, the youngest name is Ethalinda Martha Mandosa. My will is further that my daughter Mary Tayler Huff have my negro woman, Beck, as she is now getting in years, I will her to them above the share that I have given them in the land. My will further is that my two youngest children viz: Madora Harwell and Ethalinda Martha Mandosa Harwell, have my other five negroes viz: Hanna, Mary, Williford, Frances and Lewis. These negroes to be equally divided between them when Madora becomes of age or marrys. My will is that Commissioners be appointed by court to divide these negroes between them equally, according to their value. I mean the negroes and their increase as the case may be. My will is that the five negroes and their increase, I give it in this way to them, I mean Madora & Ethalinda Martha Madora, to them and to the heirs of their bodies, with the seven hundred and twelve dollars mentioned in the above will. My will further is that all the beds and furniture that came by my first wife, Dolly Harwell, my daughter Mary Tayler have and all the beds and furniture that I have that came by my last wife Mary Harwell, to be given equally between my two youngest children, Madora & Ethelinda Martha Mandosa. My will is that the negroes that I have given to my two youngest children be hired privately by my executors untill they become of age and the money arising from the hire of the negroes go for the support and schooling of them, to be put out at interest by my executors, also my will further is that all of my property not mentioned in this will be sold to the highest bidder on a twelve months credit, have and approved security, by my executors. My will further is that all my just debts be paid. Now should there not be money enough ariving from the sale of the property that is not willed to pay off my debts, my will is that my three childrens shares be drawn out of equally, untill my debts are all settled. My will further is that my grave and my last wife's and two children be all walled in together with

/rock

and paid out of my estate.

I hereby appoint my son in law William B. Huff and Samuel Sherrel to be my executors to this my last will and testament, and I solemnly declair this to be my own will and last testament. In testimony whereof, I hereunto set my hand and seal the day and date above written.

G.M. HARWELL (Seal)

Attest.
Joseph McCoy
William Young, Sen.

SALLY HARWELL

WILL 1841

In the name of God, Amen.

I, Sally Harwell, being of sound & disposing mind and memory, do make & publish this my last will and testament in manner and form following: Hereby revoking all other wills heretofore made by me.

Item 1st. I give and bequeath to my neice, Ann Eliza Wells, one negro girl named Wincey.

Item 2nd. I give and bequeath to my sister Nancy Wells, my riding mare called Diamond, three beds & furniture & steads, and also four trunks.

Item 3rd. I give and bequeath to my brother Hartwell Harwell, a note which I hold on him for about two hundred dollars.

Item 4th. I give and bequeath to my neice, Caroline McKnight, the sum of two hundred dollars. My desire and will is that her father Robert McKnight shall have no control over it whatever, and I therefore desire that Amasa Ezell be appointed to be her guardian to manage it for her, till she becomes twenty one years of age or marries, and if she should die before she becomes of lawful age or marries, my will is that the two hundred dollars which I have herein above given to her, shall be then given to my nephew James B. Wells.

Item 5th. I give and bequeath further to my nephew James B. Wells, one year old colt & one bureau.

Item 6th. I give and bequeath to my neice, Sarah C. Wells, my sorrel colt, named Hard times.

Item 7th. I give and bequeath to my neice Sarah Harwell, daughter of Hartwell Harwell, one bureau & my flowered trunk.

Item 8th. I give and bequeath to my sister, Nancy Wells, all the residue and remainder of my estate, real and personal, except so much thereof as may be necessary to pay my just debts, and defraying my funeral expenses.

Lastly, & Mainly I hereby nominate & appoint William D. Abernathy, executor of this my last will and testament.

In witness whereof, I have hereunto set my hand and seal this 17th. day of April 1841.

SALLY HARWELL (Seal)

Signed, sealed and delivered
in presence of
F. E. Phelps
Ramulus S. Swift, Jurat
William Rainey, Jurat

SAMUEL HARWELL

WILL 1837

In the name of God, Amen.

In the year of our Lord, one thousand eight hundred and thirty seven I, Samuel Harwell, being weak in body, but sound in mind do make this my last will and testiment. I appoint my Executors to sell my two old negroes, Will and Jane, said negroes shall choose the purchasers and they shall be valued to them at a fair price.

I appoint my Executors to sell all my perishable property, as stock, household and kitchen furniture and my present crop, except what I gave to my children and my grandson, John T. Harwell, four hundred dollars when comes of age, the balance of the sale with other money due me to be equally divided between my children. I give my son, Robert M. Harwell & Wm. S. Harwell all my land to be equally divided between them, when they come of age. I give my son Robert M. Harwell, two negroes, viz; Joe and Liza, a horse, bridle and saddle and a bedstead and furniture when he comes of age.

I give my daughter, Museadora A. Harwell, three negroes, Jimmy,Daniel and Sally, a gray mare, bridle and saddle A bedstead and furniture, when she comes of age. I give my son, William S. Harwell, three negroes, vis; Jacob, Jesse and Cinda, a gray horse which he now claims, bridle, and saddle and a bedstead and furniture, when he comes of age. I give my daughter, S. Caroline Harwell, three negroes, Mike, Harvey and Crease, a horse, bridle, saddle, and bedstead and furniture, when she becomes of age. I give my grandson, John T.R. Harwell, a horse, bridle, and saddle to be valued at one hundred dollars, a bedstead and furniture when he comes of age. I appoint Coleman Harwell, & Levi Sherrel, my executors, this 20th of July 1837.

SAMUEL HARWELL (Seal)

Tests.
James McKnight, Jurat
Peter Mays, Jurat

SAMUEL HARWELL.

WILL 1849

I, Samuel Harwell, do make and publish this, my last will and testament, thereby revoking all others by me made at any time.

First, I direct that my funeral expenses and all my just debts be paid as soon after my death as possible, out of any money that I may be possessed of or may first come into the hands of my Executor or Executors.

Secondly, I give unto my son, Frederick, the tract of land with all the appertains, thereunto belonging, on which he now resides known as the Davis place.

Thirdly, I give and bequeath unto my son, John the tract of land on which he now resides, with all the appertains thereunto belonging with the same of three hundred dollars in money.

Fourthly, I give and bequeath unto my son, James and William C. the tract of land on which they now reside to be equally divided between them, with all the appertances thereunto belonging.

Fifthly, I give and bequeath unto my dear wife and Thomas, the tract of land on which I now reside, with all the appertances thereunto belonging to be solely Thomas' at the death of my wife, Nancy.

Sixthly. I give and bequeath unto my dear wife, Nancy my girl Mary, a slave during her natural life or widowhood.

Seventhly, The remainder of my slaves, I give and bequeath unto my children to be equally divided among them.

Eighthly, The ballance of my effects I desire to be sold and divided equally between my dear wife, Nancy, my sons, Mason, Frederick, John, James, William C. & Thomas, and my daughter, Susan Crowder, and to the end I do hereby nominate and appoint Samuel G. Buchanan and John Harwell, as Executors of this my last will and testament. In witness whereof, I hereunto set my hand and seal the 17th day of September, 1849.

his
SAMUEL X HARWELL (Seal)
mark

Signed, sealed and published in our presence and we have subscribed our names hereto in the presence of the testator, the day and date above written.
Rufus F. Buchanan, Jurat
Ambrose Harwell, Jurat

MARIAH HAWKINS

WILL 1839

I, Mariah Hawkins, of Elkton, Giles County and State of Tennessee, being of sound mind and memory do make this my last will & testament.
Item: I loan to my sister Elizabeth Jones Harwood, my negroes, Spence, Lucy and Margarette, and their labor, during her life and then I give them to her children.
Item: I give to my nephew, John S. Hawkins, my houses and lots in Elkton, and all my lands on the other side of Elk River, also all the balance of my negroes, not before or herein to be willed, except Caroline and little Mingo, also my household and kitchen furniture (including my books) excepting side board and bureau, also all of my stock of horses, cattle & hogs, my carriage, wagon, & plantation tools, also my gold watch chains &.
Item: I loan to Harriett M. Harris, my negroes, Caroline & little Mingo, during her life, and at her death, I give them to her children.
Item: I give to my sister, Elizabeth Jones Harwood, six new silver teaspoons, now in my house.
Item: I give to my sister, Sarah Massey, my side board.
Item: It is my desire that my nephew, John L. Hawkins, have a plain neat tomb put over me, and my deceased husband.
Item: I appoint my nephew, John L. Hawkins, sole Executor, of this my last will and testament, who is authorized to collect all monies due me, pay all my debts, and the balance I give him.
In testimony whereof, I have hereunto set my hand & seal this the 23rd, of January 1839.

MARIA HAWKINS (Seal)

Witness.
James Abernathy, Jurat
James Long, Jurat
George D. Scruggs, Jurat

BENJAMIN F. HENDERSON

WILL 1849

In the name of God, Amen.

I, Benjamin Franklin Henderson, of the County of Giles & State of Tennessee, considering the uncertainity of this mortal life and being of sound mind & memory, do make and publish this my last will and testament in manner and form following, (that is to say)

First, I give and bequeath my body to the grave and my soul to the God, who gave it, and

Second, it is my wish tha all my just debts be paid out of any money that may come into the hands of my executor.

Item: I give & bequeath all my property to my beloved wife to have and to hold, during her widowhood or natural life, and in case of the marriage of my wife, then the property is to be divided into five equal parts, my wife is to have and to hold, one share, to dispose of as she may choose, & in case of the death of either of my children, then those that survive shall be considered heirs to the deceased.

Item: I wish my Executor to sell so much of my crops & other perishable property as will be nessary to pay all my just debts.

Item: If my wife should not be disposed to remain on my farm, then the executor shall have power to sell or dispose of it as he may think best, and lastly, it is my wish that my brother, James Henderson shall act as my Executor, to this my last will and testament. In witness whereof, I have set my hand and seal this seventh day of January, 1849.

his
BENJAMIN X F. HENDERSON
mark

Sealed, signed and published in
our presence and we have subscribed
our names hereto in the presence of
the testators, this 7th January 1849

Tests:
A.J. Watkins, Jurat
William Hunnicutt, Jurat
Samuel M. Ewing, Jurat
Geo. T.M. Vance, Jurat

NANCY L.C. HENDERSON

WILL 1849

Know all men by these that I, N. Lucinda C. Henderson, being weak in
body and of feeble health, but of sound mind and memory, blessed be the
name of God, have this day made and published this my last will and testament as follows:

First, I will and desire that all my just debts be paid and that such
just debts as remain due & payable to me should be collected and applied
to the payment of my debts, and that if there should be any residue, after
paying my debts, such residue be equally divided between my mother and
sister, Mary C. Stratton.

Second: I will and bequeath unto my beloved mother, whose kindest
care and support I have ever received, both in sickness & health, my negro
boy, Mark, a slave for life.

Third, I will and bequeath unto my beloved sister, Mary C. Stratton
my negro man, Addison, a slave for life.

Fourth: It is my will and desire and I do so direct that my undivided
tract of land lying in civil district No. 17, of Giles County, Tennessee
of which my father died seized and possessed of should be divided into
three equal shares & that one share be given to my beloved brother, William
J. Henderson, one share to my beloved sister, Jane N. Hurt, and one share
to the children of my deceased sister, Malissa E. Massey, but it is my will
and desire if my beloved sister, Jane N. Hurt should depart this life without disposing of her said share of the land, that her share should then
be equally divided between Mary C. Stratton, W.J. Henderson, and the children of Malissa E. Massey, the children to take one third in place of their
mother.

Fifth: But if the negro man Addison, above bequeathed to my sister
Mary C. Stratton, should die or become disabled by sickness before a
division of said land shall take place, I then and in that case, I will
and bequeath unto my beloved sister, Mary C. Stratton and equal share in
my fathers tract of land, or the proceeds thereof, when sold. In that
case, the interest which I have in said land will be devided into four
equal shares.

Sixth: I will and desire that my beloved brother, William J. Henderson
whose face I may never behold in this world, be appointed my Executor to
execute and perform this my last will and testament.

Witness my hand and seal this 27th day of February, 1849, the word
case interlined before signing.

N.L.C. HENDERSON (Seal)

Signed, sealed and published by
the above named
N.L.C. Henderson, in our presence
and witnessed by us at her request
on the said 27th day of Feb. 1849
Tests:
James S. Haynes, Milton A. Haynes, Jurat
Dorinda J. Marsh
Maria M. Pillow

WILLIAM HENDERSON

WILL 1829

In the name of God, Amen.

I, William Henderson, being weak of body, but of sound mind and memory do make and ordain this my last will & testament. In the first place it is my will that all my just debts (which are but few) be paid as soon as possible.

To my beloved wife, Eleanor, I lend for the term of five years or during her natural life or widowhood the plantation on which now live, (except what is hereafter mentioned) also all my plantation utensils of every kind, and all my household and kitchen furniture, and all my stock of horses, (except one bay horse, hereafter mentioned) and all my stock and cattle & hogs &. of every description for the purpose of making a support for herself & my four children, towit: John J., Nancy C., Jane M. & Mary P. Henderson & giving to such of them as may yet need a competant education all sharing as their various minstery may require during the said term of four years. At the expiration of said term (or at the death or marriage of my beloved wife, Eleanor) the said land and various effects before mentioned are to be equally divided, either by sale or otherwise as a majority of S. legities may desire, allowing an equal share to my beloved wife Eleanor (should she then be living) with my son, John J. & my four daughters, Lucinda M. Cravin, Nancy C., Jane M., & Mary P. Henderson after deducting the sums that have already been advanced, towit, from my daughters, Lucinda M. Cravin, sum of two hundred dollars, from my son, John J. the sum of two hundred dollars, from my daughter, Nancy C. the sum of one hundred dollars, to my daughter Sarah Marlow, I give and bequeath the sum of five dollars as I have heretofore given her a full share.

To my son, John J. I give and bequeath one bay horse (known by the name of Jim).

To John W. Weis, I give and bequeath the sum of ten dollars when he shall have come of age.

It is farther my will and desire that my Executor hereafter named when ever he shall judge it for the interest of my family to cause to be laid out and at his discression to sell any number of lots adjoining the town now laid out on my said farm afforesaid that he may deem necessary for the extention of said town & he is hereby authorised to sell and make title to the same, & also to sell two remaining lots in said town No.------ and apply the proceeds of said lots to the support & use of my beloved wife, Eleanor & my children aforesaid.

I hereby constitute and appoint my trusty friend, Ephriam Massey, Executor to this my last will and testament.

In witness whereof, I have hereunto set my hand and seal this 27th November 1829., In presence of testators.

W. HENDERSON, (Seal)

Tests,
Jno. M. Patrick, J.
Moses Hoge, J.

ANDREW J. HICKMAN

WILLS 1852

I, Andrew J. Hickman, do make and publish this my last will and testament.

First. my will and desire is that all my debts and funeral expenses, be paid out of the first money that comes into the hands of my Executor.

Second, My will and desire is that my wife, Mary and all my family together with my father, Samuel Hickman, shall remove to the tract of land on Fountain Creek, Maury County, Tennessee which I purchased of James H. Emmen,

Third, my will is that my said wife, during her widowhood shall live on said land and support my said father & mother and raise my three children, towit, James Calvin, John Gilbreath and Andrew Jackson, and the proceeds arising from farming and tilling said land, shall be appropriated to the education of said children after a sufficiency is appropriated to the support of the family, and if there should be any money arising from said farm, after educating the children, I desire it to go into the hands of my executors.

Fourth, If my said wife should not marry untill my youngest child, Andrew Jackson, arives at the age of twenty one years, then I desire that there be an equal division between my three children and her of all my estate, but if she should marry before that time, then I desire her to have five hundred dollars only in cash and her saddle and one bed and furniture and the balance of my estate to be equally divided between my three children.

Fifth, if either of my three children should die without issue, then my will is that the other two children shall heir its portion equally.

Sixth, If my said wife should marry prior to the death of my father and mother, then I desire that my wife shall leave the place and my father and mother remain on the same and be decently supported and all the surplus proceeds to go into the hands of my executor's.

Seventh, I desire at the death of my father and mother, if that event should occur after their death or marriage of my wife, that all my property except the lands be sold on a twelve months credit to the highest bidder.

Eighth and lastly, I ordain and appoint Noah Hickman, my executor to this my last will and testament.

Given under my hand and seal this the 9th. day of October A.D. 1852.

ANDREW J. HICKMAN

Test.

W.L. Willeford, Jurat
I.B. Galbreath
Jesse D. Whitman, Jurat

SAMUEL HICKMAN

WILLS 1850

State of Tennessee)
Giles, County   )

I, Samuel Hickman, Sr. do make and publish this my last will and testament, hereby revoking and making void all other wills by me at any time made.

First, I direct that my funeral expenses and all my debts which I owe be paid as soon after my death as possible, out of any money that I may die possessed of, or that may first come into the hands of my Executors.

Secondly, I give and bequeath to my well beloved wife, Nancy, during her life, two feather beds and furniture, cupboard, chest, and all other articles, belonging to the house.

Thirdly, I have heretofore given to my son, John an amount equal to what I shall be able to give each of my other sons, which I hereby make my bequest in full to him.

Fourthly, I give to my son, William a twenty four dollar note, which I hold against him. I also give him seventy six dollars in full of his portion of my estate.

Fifthly, I have heretofore given to my son Samuel, an amount equal to what I shall be able to give each of my other sons, which I hereby make my bequest in full to him.

Sixthly, I give to my son Noah, a ten dollar due/bill which I hold against him. I also give to him ninety dollars in full, of his portion of my estate.

Seventhly: I give to my son Jesse D. two notes, one of sixty five dollars & 26 cents, and the other of ten dollars which I hold against him. I also give him twenty four dollars & 74 cents, in full of his portion of my estate.

Eighthly, I have heretofore given to my son, Snodon, an amount equal to what I shall be able to give each of my other sons, I hereby make my bequest in full, to him.

Ninthly: I have heretofore given to my son, Andrew J. three hundred dollars for the maintenance of me and my wife, Nancy, during our natural lives. I have also given unto him, one hundred dollars in full his portion of my estate.

Tenthly: I give to my five daughters, Elizabeth, Mary, Lucinda, Avy and Nancy, all the balance of my property, be it of whatever nature or kind, to be sold at my death and equally divided among them, among them. Also all the articles which I have given to my wife at her death to be sold and equally divided among my five daughters aforesaid.

Lastly, I nominate and appoint my two sons, Noah & Andrew J. Hickman, my whole & sole executors of this my last will and testament.

In witness whereof I have hereunto set my hand and affixed my seal, this the twenty first day of March, A.D. Eighteen hundred and fifty,

SAMUEL HICKMAN (Seal)

Signed, sealed and acknowledged in
presence of,
Hardy Willsford, Jurat
William S. Willsford, Jurat

The words "during her life" above the eleventh line on first page interlined before assignment.

JOHN HIGDON

WILLS 1835

In the name of God, Amen.

I, John Higdon, of Giles County and State of Tennessee, of sound mind and memory, blessed be God, do this day make my last will and testament in manner and form following, viz;

I have given my son, James Eaton Higdon, one horse, my will is that he shall have seventy dollars because of his affection, which money is to be paid out of my estate, on the twenty fifth day of December 1836.

I have given my daughter, Elizabeth Briant Moore, one bed and furniture & one cow and calf, and my will is that my daughter, Elizabeth shall have forty dollars, paid her, because of her affection, paid on the twenty fifth day of December, 1836.

I have given my daughter Jane Swanson Maxey, one bed and furniture, and one cow and calf, and my will is that she shall be paid, twenty dollars, out of my estate because of her affection, said money to be paid on the twenty fifth day of December 1826.

I have given to my son, Larkin Lanier Higdon, one horse.

I have given to my daughter, Nancy N. Creath Higdon, when she shall become of lawful age or marries, shall have one bed & furniture, and one cow and calf.

My will is that my son John Brantley Higdon, shall at the age of twenty one years, have a horse worth seventy dollars.

My will is that Allen Hill Higdon, shall at the age of twenty one years have a horse, worth seventy dollars.

My will is that my son David K. Higdon, shall at the age of twenty one years have a horse worth seventy dollars, the above named being my eight children, whom are my lawful heirs.

My will is that my beloved wife, Anna Higdon, have and possess as a loan all my estate after the above named amounts are paid out, during her natural life ot widowhood, then to be divided equally among my children.

I also will and desire my executors, to this my last will to keep for the use of my beloved wife, the tract of land, crop, stock, household & kitchen furniture, provided there be a sufficiency of money after all, my just debts are paid, and my money I have willed to my dear children.

And my will and desire is, that should any of the children be afflicted hereafter under the age of twenty five that then & in that case, they being afflicted shall receive in proportion to those already provided for (because of affliction)

I do hereby make and ordain my son, Larkin Lanier Higdon, and my son in law, Isaih T. Maxey Executors of this my last will and testament.

In witness whereof, I hereunto set my hand and affix my seal, this 24th day of December, 1835. Written and interline before assigned.

JOHN HIGDON (Seal)

Witness,
George Malone
Allen Hill

Codicil:
My will is that my beloved wife, Anna Higdon, have priveledge to sell

my land and lay out the money for other lands where she may wish to reside
& although it is a loan as written in the body of this my last will and
testament, yet notwithstanding, my will is that her title in case she
should sell & purchase elsewhere be lawful.

        This codicil was written & interlined, before assigned, on the twenty
fourth day of December 1835.

                                        JOHN HIGDON (Seal)

Tests.
George Malone
Allen Hill

DAVID HILL
WILL 1851

I, David Hill, do make and publish this my last will and testament, hereby revoking and making void all other will by me at any time made.

First, I direct that my funeral expences and all my debts be paid as soon after my death as possible out of any moneys that I may die possessed of or may first come into the hands of my executor.

Secondly, I give and bequeath to my beloved wife, Martha J. Hill and the heirs of her body, all my possessions consisting of my farm on which I live and a small tract on the ridge, farming utencils, househould and kitchen furniture, stockn and my boy Ramond, Nancy and Drucila, negro slaves.

Lastly, I do hereby nominate and appoint Milton McClure my executor.

In witness whereof, I do to this my last will, set my hand and seal this 27th day of January 1851.

DAVID HILL (Seal)

Signed, sealed and published
in our presence and we have
subscribed our names., hereto in
the presence of the testator, this
January 27th. 1851
Y.M. Hudson (Seal)
David B. Pickens (Seal)

DAVID HOGAN .

WILL 1834

In consideration of the certainity of death, an event that happens to all flesh, and of the uncertainity of the time at which such event might take place, I David Hogan, of the County of Giles and State of Tennessee, do make and ordain this my last will and testament in which I make the following disposition of my estate both real and personal towit;

As my estate is small and would not be of much value equally divided among all my children but would be of value to one alone, therefore for services done and to be done, I give and bequeath to my son, Wiley G. Hogan, the whole of my estate, both real and personal to have and to hold for his own use and benefit at my decease, and for the due and faithful execution of this my last will I do appoint James Jones of the County and State aforesaid, my Executors and he is hereby authorised, amaediately after my decease to put this my will in due execution according to the disposition above written.

Furthermore, I do revoke and make null and void all other will or wills by me made, and ordain this my last will.

In testimony whereof I have hereunto set my hand and affixed my seal this 24th day of October in the year of our Lord one thousand eight hundred and thirty four.

                                        His
                              DAVID X HOGAN
                                        Mark

Signed in presence of
Ezekiel Springer, Jurat
Ross Tompenson, Jurat

C.M. HOLLOWELL

WILL 1860

I, Caroline M. Hollowell, do make and declare this my last will and testament, revoking & making void all other wills made by me at any previous time.

First, I direct that my funeral expenses & all my legal debts be paid as soon after my death as possible, and of such monies as I may be possessed of or that may come into the hands of my executors.

Secondly, I request that my executor, erect at the expense of my estate a handsome marble couch, over the remains of my late husband, Dr. John Hollowell & that his grave be enclosed with a neat substantial iron railing.

Thirdly, I give and bequeath to my brother Dr. Samuel R. Skillern, during his natural life, and at his death to his children the following negroes, viz: Henry & Amanda, his wife, also Augusta & Amanda's youngest child. I also wish above mentioned negroes secured to Dr. Samuel Skillern & his heirs forever. Should Dr. S.R. Skillern die without heirs, these negroes, Henry, Amanda, her youngest child & Augustus are to revert to my surviving Brothers and Sisters.

Fourthly: I give and bequeath to my beloved Martha B. Skillern, all the remainder of my property real & personal & mixed. I have a few small mementoes which I have requested her to distribute among my friends. Should my brother, Claud Hollowell Skillern survive my mother, Mrs. M.B. Skillern I wish her to secure the negro boy, Andrew, now about 14 years of age to said C.H. Skillern. I do hereby nominate my friend Thomas Martin, my Executor.

In witness whereof I herewith affix my hand and seal this the 11th day of May 1857.

                                        CARRIE M. HOLLOWELL (Seal)

Witnesses:
Mrs. A.P. Skillern
John C. Holloway

Since the foregoing will was written, my brother Dr. Samuel R. Skillern, having removed to a non slave holding State, becomes unqualified to own slaves, therefore I revoke the bequest (of negroes) made in his favor & hereby bequeath to my beloved mother Mrs. M.B. Skillern during her life, all property which may remain to my estate after my just & legal debts shall have been paid, including my funeral expenses, & the marble monument & iron railing directed to be placed over & around the grave of my beloved husband, Dr. John T. Hollowell & a sum of five hundred , which I wish given and secured to my neice Carrie H. Winslow, in case she should survive me, should Jas. A.P. Skillern continue kind & affectionate to my dear Mother, Mrs. M.B. Skillern, I wish her to bequeath him, Augustus, whom he shall hold as a slave on the condition of his proving & continuing a kind master to the said Augustus, otherwise he forfeits this claim at the death of my mother, which I pray a merciful Heaven will long avert the small amount of property inherited by her from me, should be equally divided between my surviving brothers & Sister.

To this Codicil I herewith affix my hand and seal this the eighth day of November, A.D. 1860.

                                        CARRIE M. HOLLOWELL (Seal)

ENOCH E. HOLT

WILL 1857

I, Enoch E. Holt, of Giles County & State of Tennessee, being of sound mind and memory and in good health, and knowing the uncertainity of life and the ccartainity of death do make and publish this as my last will and testament, hereby revoking and making void all other wills by me at any time made.

First, I direct that mt funeral expences and all my just debts be paid as soon after my death as possible, out of any money that I may die possessed of or may first come into the hands of my Executor.

Secondly, I give and bequeath to my beloved wife, Mary Ann Holt, all the property I now have or may hereafter acquire of any kind, and description both real and personal, to be by her used and disposed of in any manner, she may see proper, but if I shall hereafter have any children by my present wife, then in that event it is my will and I hereby direct that each of my children shall have an equal share of all my property of every kind, with my wife, Mary Ann Holt,. I do hereby nominate and appoint my wife, Mary Ann Holt, my Executrix. In witness whereof I do to this my last will and testament set my hand and seal this the 19th day of October in the year of our Lord one thousand eight hundred and fifty seven.

Interlination between the eighth and ninth line, my present wife made before signing.

ENOCH E. HOLT (Seal)

Signed, sealed and published
in our presence & we have subscribed our
names in the presence of the testator
& at his request this 19th October 1857

John C. Walker
John C. Brown

Monday 8th Junen 1857.

This is to certify that I, William H. Howard, being of sound mind do hereby make and publish this as my last will and testament, hereby revoking and making void all other wills by me at any time made.

First, I direct that mt funeral expences and all my debts be paid as soon after my death as possible, out of any money that I may die possessed of or may first come into the hands of my executors.

Secondly, I give and bequeath to my son, Benjamin Adams, a negro boy named Jim Polk and a horse too, worth one hundred and fifty dollars, which will make him as near equal with what I have given my son, Robert, and my daughter, Margaret, as I can estimate the said boy and horse, however are to remain in possession of my wife, Martha B. Howard, until my son Benjamin completes the study of medicine and locates.

Thirdly, I give and bequeath to my wife, Martha B. Howard, all the balance of my property, towit, negro man Charles, negro man, Ambrose, boy Calhoun, boy, Jim Adam, negro woman Milly, and her three youngest children namely, Scott, Polly, Ann & Brickenridge, negro woman Agnes, and her three children namely, Pierce, Hannah and Parthena, negro woman, Elsie, negro girl, Lucy and the increases of said negroes during her life. After her death the said negroes and their increase are to be equally divided among my children by her. I however leave it at her option to give or not the children their proportionable part of the property as they marry or become of age as she may think best.

Furthermore, I give and bequeath to my wife, Martha B. Howard all my horses, hogs, cows, sheep, plantation tools, household and kitchen furniture, as well as allother property not here in embraced that I may possess to have and dispose of just as she chooses.

My son, Robert and my daughter Margaret Ann, having been the children of another wife, whose property they heired and have now in possession besides have given Robt. of my own property a negro man named Davy, and a horse and my daughter, Margaret Ann, a negro woman named Rachel, and her child named Fillmore, and a horse and I do not think that my present property will be more to each child than what I have already given to my son, Robt. Benjamin and my daughter, Margaret Ann, this much is added by way of explanation to avoid any appearance of parshality, all my children being equally dear to me.

Last, I do nominate and appoint Thomas D. Deavenport as my Executor. In witness whereof, I do to this my last will and testament set my hand and seal this the eighth day if June eighteen hundred and fifty seven.

                                        WM. H. HOWARD (Seal)

Signed, sealed and published
in our presence and we have
subscribed our names hereunto
in the presence of the testators
this the 8th June, 1857
Test.
Wm. I. Craig
A.J. Gilmore

47

ZEALOUS HOWELL

WILL 1854

June the 25th 1854.

My will is that enough of my property be sold such as can be spared
best, and my just debts paid, then I lend the balance to my wife, stock
and land during her widowhood or until the youngest child comes of age,
with the exception of the newground, when Edwin comes of age. If he
marry's or wants to settle he has the liberty of the new ground and if
not let the mother and children tend it untill he does want it and when
the youngest child comes of age, I give one horse to my youngest son
Henry and the balance to be divided among all my heirs except Edwin, after
leaving a suffience for support and welfare of the mother, and if she
should marry let all the heirs have their full rights, and at the direction let Edwin have another field, and after the widowhood or death of the
mother, I give the land to my second son Edwin, and the remaining property
to be divided among all the heirs and let it be considered that the land
is not to be sold, no part of it, untill the death of the mother, for it
with the stock and other property, for the support of the mother, and if
she continue a widow and Edwin, I want you to take account of your mother
in her old age, but it be considered that I want the young ones sent to
school, as much as can be well be spared. I leave John B. Hudson, to
settle my debts.

                                          ZEALOUS HOWELL

                              fee not paid

Henry Morris
Lovell B. Coffman

I, Rebecca Huff, of the County of Giles and of the State of Tennessee, do make and publish this my last will and testament in manner following, viz:

1st. It is my will and I do direct that my executors as soon after my decease as may be practicable, pay all my just debts out of the first available monies of my estate that came to hand.

2nd. Whereas my sons, Sterling Huff, Pinckney Huff & Daniel Huff and Wiley Huff, became indebted to me for monies loaned, I therefore give unto each one of them the amount of money due me from each of them as their part of my estate.

I also give to my son William Huff, five dollars, and to the heirs of my eldest daughter, Sarah Bennett, I give five dollars to be divided among the said heirs and I also give unto the heirs of my youngest son Early Huff, deceased, five dollars, also to be divided among said heirs, which money is to be paid over to each person and in amount as is herein specified, by my executors, after my decease.

3rd. I give to my youngest and only daughter, Permelia Jackson Pentecost, wife of William H. Pentecost, the following negroes herein named, Fanny, Sylvia & Sarah with all their increase, Robert and Jesse, during her natural life, and at her death said negroes and their increase to be equally divided according to valuation among the heirs of her body, and whereas, I sold a certain negro man, for the sum of nine hundred and fifty dollars, with the intention of purchasing another negro. Now if I should not in my life time purchase another negro, them I give unto her my said daughter, Permelia Jackson Pentecost, the above named sum, of nine hundred and fifty dollars, which money I hereby direct to be laid out in the purchase of a negro for her, my said daughter, Permelia Jackson Pentecost, to be hers during her natural life and at her death with the above named negroes to be equally divided among the heirs of her body.

I also give to my said daughter, Permelia Jackson Pentecost, all my stock of horses, cattle, sheep, and hogs, also all my household and kitchen furniture and plantation utensils. I also give to her, the said Permelia Jackson Pentecost, that portion of the track of land whereon I now live which I purchased of my son, Sterling Huff, which was his proportional part of said tract of land which he drew in the division of land.

4th. I appoint David Crook sole Executor to this my last will and testament.

In testimony whereof, I have hereunto set my hand and affixed my seal this the alst day of October in the year of our Lord one thousand eight hundred and fifty five.

her

REBECCA X HUFF (Seal)

mark

Signed and sealed
in the presence of
Turner Abernathy.

I, Rebecca Huff, of the County of Giles, and State of Tennessee, do

make and publish this codicil to my will and Testament, whereas it is
mentioned in this my will and testament the sale of a certain negro man
for the sum of nine hundred and fifty dollars, with a view to purchasing
another negro, and having purchased in my life time another negro man,
named Charels, I therefore give unto my above named daughter, Permelia
Jackson Pentecost, said negro man named Charles, during her natural life
at her death with other negroes mentioned to be equally divided among all
of the heirs of her body.

In testimony whereof I have hereunto set my hand & seal this 18th.
January A.D. 1857.

                                        her
                              REBECCA X HUFF
                                        mark

Signed & sealed in
the presence of
Rebecca mark Crook
John H. Loyd
Stephen C. Loyd

STERLING HUFF

WILL 1855

In the name of God, Amen.

This 29th day of January in the year of our Lord, eighteen hundred and fifty five, I, Sterling Huff of the State of Tennessee and County of Giles being very sick and weak in body but of perfect and sound mind and memory and calling to mind the mortality of my body and knowing that it is appointed for all to die, do make and ordain this my last will and testament, that is to say principally and first of all, I give and recommend my soul into the hands of God that gave it and my body I recommend it to the earth to be buried in a Christain like manner, and as touching such worldly estate wherewith it hath pleased God to give me in this life I give and dispose of the same in the manner and form following.

First, that my land where I now live and my negro boy, Robert and all the balance of my property that is not mentioned in this my last will and testament for my executor to take charge of, during my wife, Susan G. Huff's widowhood ot untill my youngest child becomes to the age of sixteen years, his name is Permelia Huff, and she was born on the 23 day of February 1851, or untill my daughter Permilia Huff marries. My will is that my wife and children that are not married are to remain on the land and farm where I now live and be supported by the farm or off the farm on which I now live and also to have my named children educated and my negro boy Robert to remain with my family and his labour in like manner with the land and farm. Further, my will is that my executor take charge and manage the property above specified for the better mantainance of my wife Susan G. Huff and unmarried children up to the time above mentioned.

I further will that my buggy and buggy horse and one other horse and two yoke of oxen and a lot of bacon to be sold on a twelve months credit with bond and approved security.

I further will that an equal division be made of all my property herein willed between my wife, Susan G. Huff and my nine children, that is, I mean that my wife is to have a child's part with my nine children, towit: Mary Ann Gwin, Martha G. McLaurine, William G. Huff, Rebecca Young, Elizabeth J. Huff, James Valentine Huff, Nancy A. Huff, Virginia F. Huff, and Permelia Huff, and I hereby appoint William Young Senior to be my Executor to this my last will and testament and I solemnly declair, this to be my own will and last testament, in testimony whereof, I hereunto set my hand and seal the day and date above mentioned.

STERLING HUFF? (Seal)

G.B. SUTTON
WILLIAM WORLEY

LOUIS HUNNICUTT

WILL 1860

I, Louis Hunnicutt do make and publish this as my last will and testament, hereby revoking and making void all other wills by me at any time made.

First. I direct that my funeral expences and all my debts be paid as soon after my death as possible, out of any moneys that I may die possessed of, or may first come into the hands of my executors.

Secondly. I want my soul to go to my Maker, and my body to the ground I wish to be buried in a plain, simple manner in my own garden on the corner of the second square to the right of the walk that leads from the gate.

Thirdly. I give to my nephews, Hiram T. Hunnicutt, Winfield S. Hunnicutt, & Wesley White Hunnicutt, each one thousand dollars.

Fourthly. I give to my nephews, George Buchanan Hunnicutt and James Washington Hunnicutt, sons of my brother Roland Hunnicutt, deceased, who reside in the State of Texas, each five hundred dollars.

Fifthly; I give to my neice, Elizabeth Jane Hunnicutt, daughter of my aforesaid brother, Roland, one thousand and five hundred dollars, and my gold watch and rigging, which legacy I want so secured to her that it will not be squandered by her husband if she should marry.

Sixthly. I give to my neice Jane Jackson, daughter of William & Polly Lamm, one thousand dollars. I also give to my nephew, Malcolm Lamm, son of the aforesaid William & Polly Lamm, one thousand dollars.

Seventhly. I give to my nephew, Adolphus Franklin Coldwell, and James Buchanon Coldwell each one thousand dollars.

Eighthly. I give to my sister, Sarah C. Coldwell, my negro woman, Milly and my negro girl Harriett, during her lifetime, and at her death I want her children to have them. I hope also that the said negro woman Milly, will be treated kindly, and have as much liberty as is consistent with the laws of the land. I also give in trust, to my brother in law, James Coldwell, two hundred dollars ($200.00) for the purpose of using for the comfort of the said servant Milly, by furnishing a house and garden for her, and procuring for her, whatever else her comfort may require.

I desire that Hiram T. Hunnicutt, whom I will hereinafter appoint one of my Executors, shall also retain my cow and calf and one hundred dollars out of the remaining portion of my estate, for the sole use of my said servant, Milly, to be given to her as her needs require it, and also that he the said Hiram T. Hunnicutt, shall retain one other hundred dollars, to be given to my servant Harriett in like manner.

Ninthly. I give to my brother, Anthony Hunnicutt, five hundred dollars,

Tenthly. I give to my nephew Hiram T. Hunnicutt, my store house and lots and parts of lots lying contiguous thereto in the town of Elkton, Giles County, Tennessee, for and in consideration of his trouble in assisting to execute my will, and supporting my mother her lifetime.

Eleventhly. I give the remainder of my estate real, personal, and mixed to my brother, William Hunnicutt, my sister, Polly Lamm and my sister Sarah Coldwell, to be divided equally among them.

Lastly, O do hereby nominate and appoint Hiram T. Hunnicutt and my brother, William Hunnicutt, my Executors.

In witness whereof, I do to this my will set my hand & seal this the
11th. day of July, 1849.

LOUIS HUNNICUTT (Seal)

Signed, sealed and published
in our presence, and we have
subscribed our names hereto
in the presence of the testator this 11th day of July 1849.
P.H. Phelps, Jurat
Samuel M. Ewins, Jurat

ELIZABETH JOHNSTON

WILL 1848

I, Elizabeth Johnston, of the County of Giles, and State of Tennesse do make and publish this my last will and testament in manner and form following, revoking all former wills heretofore by me made, if any, and

1st. It is my will that all my just debts be paid out of the first monies arising from any portion of my estatem that may come into the hands of my executors.

2nd. I give unto my sister, Fatamy Atkins, one cow and calf.

3rd. It is my will that the balance of my stock of cattle, household and kitchen furniture be sold and the proceeds be appointed to the payment of my debts.

4th. After payment of all my just debts I give to my grand daughter Albina Franklin Johnston, all the remainder of my estate to be delivered to her when she arrives to lawful age, which consists of eleven negroes, namely, Sophia, and her six children, Kizeah and her two children, and Hannah, and should my said grand daughter Albina Franklin Johnston, die having no heirs, then in that case it is my will and I do decree that the said negroes, if they should have been delivered to her, or the proceeds from the sale of them, as will be herein afterwards directed be equally divided between all of the children of my sister, Nancy Abernathy, deceased and all of the children of my brother Samuel Croft, and if any or all of said negroes embraced in the bequest to my grand daughter Albina Franklin Johnston, should at any time after my decease desires to be sold previous to my said grand daughter arriving to lawful age, then in that case, It is my will and I do authorise my Executors to sell such for valuable consideration suffering such to choose their masters and put the monies arising from said sales, out at interest and pay the same over to my grand daughter Albina Franklin Johnston, when she arrives to lawful age.

Lastly. I appoint, constitute and ordain, P.W. Phelps, Executor to this my last will and testament.

In witness whereof I, Elizabeth Johnston, testatrix to this my last will and testament, hath hereunto set my hand and seal this 5th of August in the year of our Lord, 1848.

                                                her
                        ELIZABETH X JOHNSTON (Seal)
                                                mark

Signed, sealed and delivered
in the presence of us
David Crook, Jurat
William Atkins, Jurat

WILLIAM JOHNSTON

WILL 1840

In the Name of God, Amen.

I, William Johnston of the County of Giles and State of Tennessee on this 28th of April, in the year of our Lord, one thousand eight hundred and forty, being sound in mind, but of infirm health of body, make this my last will and testament & do hereby revoke all former wills by me made.

First of all, it is my will that all my debts and burial expences be paid out of the money that I now have on hand or that may come into the hands of my executors and executrix.

Secondly, It is my will & I do hereby provide that my land and negro property or either, shall be sold if thought advisable by my executors & executrix, if not to be divided as the law directs.

Third, It is my will & I do hereby provide that my perishable property shall remain in their hands until such time as may be thought advisable by them.

Fourth. It is my will & I do hereby provide that all my property, real and personal shall be divided equally among my heirs as the law directs, and I do hereby appoint my beloved wife Jane, and my beloved brother Joseph as executor and executrix to this my last will and testament.

Signed, sealed & delivered in person on the day and date above.

WILLIAM JOHNSTON (Seal)

H.B. Warren
F.W. King
John Montgomery

DICY JONES

WILL 1857

I, Dicy Jones do make and publish this, my last will and testament, hereby revoking and making void all other wills by me made heretofore.

First, I direct that my funeral expenses and all my debts be paid as soon after my death as possible, out of my monies that I may die possessed of or may first come into the hands of my Executor.

Secondly, I give and bequeth to Wilberry Gooch, five dollars and the balance of my property I direct to be sold and equally divided amongst the balance of my children.

Lastly, I do hereby nominate and appoint William A. Jones & Joseph H. Jones, my Executors.

In witness whereof I do to this my last will, set my hand and seal this 16th day of July 1857.

her
DICY X JONES (Seal)
mark

Signed, sealed and published in our presence, and we have suscribed our names hereto in the presence of the Testater, this 16th day of July 1857.

Test.

Hezekiah Paret

James Hanna

HEZEKIAH JONES

WILL 1859

I, Hezekiah Jones, do make & wish and publish this my last will and testament, hereby revoking and making void all wills by me made heretofore.

First. I direct that my funeral expences and all my just debts be paid as soon after my death as possible, out of my monies, that I may die possessed of or may first come into the hands of my Executors.

Secondly, I give and bequeath to my beloved wife one hundred dollars in money, and houses and farm where I now live, as much as she may wish to work, and best tools, that she may choose, also all the negroes I may have, household and kitchen furniture, all the balance of my lands rented or sold, as may seem best by my executor, all other left property, as it is my wish for my estate to be equally divided, between all of my children. As I have kept an account of what each child has received of my estate with this my will, and when my executors, I wish them to prove this to be my hand write.

Lastly, I do hereby nominate and appoint my four oldest sons my executors or any two of them, David Jefferson, Modes Larasce, Daniel Hollis and John Lewis, September 1859.

HEZEKIAH JONES (Seal)

Test
David A. Gooch, Jurat
James White, Jurat

ISAAC JONES

WILL 1846

Ariten Will and Testament

May 31st. 1846, I, Isaac Jones, do make and publish this as my last will
and testament, hereby revoking and making void all other wills by me at
any time made,

First, I direct that my just debts be paid as soon after my death as
possible out of any money that I may die possessed of or may first come
into the hands of my Executors.

Second. I give and bequeath to my wife Elizabeth all of my property
that I may have left after paying all my debts, during her lifetime or
widowhood, then for it to be equally divided amongst my children and
wife or giving her her third of the lands and other property as the lene
directs.

I allso request that my Executors sell my property to the best advantage or as they may think proper,

Lastly, I do hereby nominate and appoint D.S. Ussery, and my wife,
Elizabeth my Executors. In witness I do to this my will, set my hand
and seal.

ISAAC JONES

Test,
Richard Wilks
S.G. Calvert, Jurat
W.J. Griffis, Jurat

JAMES JONES

WILL 1844

In the Name of God, Amen.

I, James Jones, of the County of Giles & State of Tennessee, being of sound mind & disposing memory, do make and ordain this my last will and testament in which I make the following dispositions of my Estate, both real and personal, hereby revoking all other will or wills by me made.

As to my kind and loving wife & her children, they have left them a better portion for their support than I can possible give to my children for their support, and confidently believing that after my death the two families will not continue to live together as at present. I, therefore, under that belief, make the best disposition I can for the support and raising of both sets of children.

Ist. I give and bequeth to my kind wife, Elizabeth Jones, during her material life, one cow and calf, one sow and pigs, one half of the crop, whether gathered or not as the case may be, and one half of bacon or pork on hand. In case of her death or marriage, all the remains of said gift to revert & be vested in my four children to be equally divided.

2nd. The balance of my Estate, both real and personal after paying all my debts, I give and bequeth in equal portions to my four children, namely, John A., James I., Nancy L. and William R. Jones.

If my children should desire to live together and not seperate, it is my will that my land remain as at present for that purpose.

3rd. My will is that Nancy L. Jones, (my daughter) have her saddle and walnut chest, extra of her equal share as in article 2nd. in this my will.

4th. It is my will that mt four children herein named have their respective portions at their full age or marriage, as the case may be.

5th. And for the due and faithful execution of this my will, I constitute and appoint my son, John A. Jones Jr. and my faithful and trusty friend, my Executor.

In witness whereof, I have hereto set my hand & seal this 23rd day of March in the year of our Lord, one thousand eight hundred & forty four.

JAMES JONES, (Seal)

Test.
J.R. Harrison, Jurat
J.H. Fetters, Jurat
Jesse Green Brown.

WILLIAM JONES'

WILL 1831

State of Tennessee, Giles County.

To all persons to whom the presents shall come, Greetings:
Know ye that the last will and testament of William Jones, decd. that in
due form of law I do appoint my friend J.C. Hall, executer of said will
appointed.

In the Name of God, Amen

I William Jones, of Giles County and State of Tennessee, being weak in
body but of strong mind, disposition, memory and understanding, considering
the sevearity of death and the uncertainity of time, and being willing &
desirous to settle all my worldly affairs, and thereby be better prepaired
to leave this world, when it please God to call me. Therefore I make and
publish this my last will and Testament in manner and form following, to -
wit.

First, and principally, I connect my Sould into the hands of Almighty
God, and body to the earth to be decently buried at the discretion of my
Executor & dear wife, & after my burial expences & other debts shall have
been discharged, I will and Bequeth as follows:

I hereby give and bequeth to my brother, Stephen Jones, one dollar and
no more.

I hereby give and bequeth to my brother John T. Jones, one dollar and
no more.

I hereby give and bequeth to my sister, Lucey Moore one dollar and no
more.

I hereby give & bequeth to my sister, Elizabeth Faris, one dollar and
no more.

I hereby give and bequeth to my sister, Nancy J. Aderson, one dollar
and no more.

I hereby give & bequeth to my sister Polly Faris, one dollar and no
more.

To be equally divided amongst his heirs and after the above bequeth
shall have been paid and all other just debts discharged, I do hereby
will and bequeth to my dear wife, Polly Jones, the residue of my estate
and lastly I hereby constitute J.C. Hale, my executor in this my last will
and testament.

In testimony whereof I here have unto set my hand and offered my seal
this, the 29th of March 1831. Inter bound before sind.

WILLIAM JONES, (Seal)

Sined, sealed, published and declared by William Jones, that the within
named Serufees is will and Testament in the presents of us, who at his request in his presents & the presents of each other here suscribed ower
names as witness thereto.

Gustarus Angus
James P. Deans
Thomas M. Scott

ELIZABETH JORDON

WILL 1844

I, Elizabeth Jordon, do make and publish this my last will and testament, hereby revoking and making void all other wills by me at any time made.

First, I direct that my funeral expences and all my debts be paid as soon as possible out of any money that I may die possessed of or may first come into the hands of my Executors.

Secondly, My will is that my property, household and kitchen furniture of all descriptions, and all my stock of all discriptions, and my land that I now live on lying and being situated in Giles County or Bradshaw Creek, District No. 10, containing fifteen acres and 75 poles, more or less to be sold on twelve months credit.

Thirdly. I give and bequeath to the heirs of my son, John Jordon, Decd. one dollar.

Forthly. I give and bequeath to my daughter, Mary Dickey, one dollar.

Fifthly. I give and bequeath my grandson, Pleasant Harvy Jordon, one dollar.

Sixthly. I give and bequeath unto my son Archibald Moore Jordon, one dollar.

Seventhly, I give and bequeath unto my daughter, Nancy Gibson, two thirds of my estate after the distribution herein named or made.

Eighthly, I give and bequeath unto my son, William Jordon, the remainder of my estate after the above named distribution is made.

Lastly. I do hereby nominate and appoint Daniel Goodrum & A.R. Moore, my executors, In witness whereof I do to this my will set my hand and seal this the 14th of March 1844.

                                                    her
                              ELIZABETH X JORDON (Seal)
                                                    mark

Wm. D. Orr, Atest
    Signed, sealed and published
in our presence and we have subscribed our names hereto in the
presence of the testators this 14th
day of March 1844.
Wm. D. Orr (Seal)
G.L. Quarles, (Seal)
Edward Ragain, (Seal)

SAMUEL JORDON

WILL 1834

I, Samuel Jordon being of sound mind and proper recollection, do make this my last will and testament.

In the first place it is my desire that my Executor and Executrix, hereinafter named pay all my just debts.

In order to divide my Estate as fairly equally and as satisfactorily as I can, I do make the following Special Legacies to two of my children and my son in law John Hawkins, intending hereby to make them equal with what I have formerly given to my other children.

I give and bequeth to my beloved daughter, Sarah W. Jennings, and the heirs of her body, a negro girl named Betsy, same girl now in her possession.

I give and bequeth to my beloved daughter Elizabeth M. Johnson, and the heirs of her body, a negro girl named Minerva, said girl being in her possession now, I give to my son in law and friend John Hawkins, a negro girl by the name of Louisa, which girl is to be delivered by my executors and Executrix.

I give and bequeth all the balance of my estate, real and personal to my beloved wife, Elizabeth Jordon, so long as she may live and at her death to be equally divided among my children that may be living, and grandchildren in right of their parents or in the event of my wife ever getting married, it is my will that half of my Estate be divided among my children and she retain the other half as long as she may live, then to be divided as aforesaid.

It is my desire that my wife and my friends, Thomas Batle and James Abernathy act as Executrix and Executors this my last will and Testament.

SAMUEL JORDON (Seal) 1834

W.P. Richardson, J.)
George Small, J.)

SAMUEL KERCHIVAL

WILL 1843

I, Samuel Kerchival, being of sound mind and disposing memory, do make and publish the following as my last will and testament.

Item 1st. It is my will and desire that after payment of all legal & just debts and clemances against me, that all of my estate, both real and personal and mixed, be equally divided between my beloved wife, Nancy H. and our daughter, and my affecinate stepdaughter Ann Henry Neal.

Item 2nd. It is my will that the property which belongs to my affectionate stepdaughter, Ann Henry, be added to and constituted a part of my estate, and be taken into the estimation in the division above, specified.

Item 3rd. It is my will and desire that my beloved wife, Nancy H. have the control & management of all my Estate, until the Legatees & devisors shall arrive at the age of twenty one years or shall marry.

Item 4th. It is my will and desire that my beloved wife, Nancy H. shall have the privelege of selecting such part of my estate as she may desire as her part, which shall be valued to her by three or more disinterested men, which portion when so selected and valued shall belong to her & her heirs absolutely.

Item 5th. It is my will and desire that my beloved wife be appointed and she is hereby appointed my sole Executrix, without security, to carry into effect this my last will & Testament, hereby revoking all other wills.

In testimony whereof, I have hereunto set my hand and seal this 21st of July 1843.

SAMUEL KERCHIVAL (Seal)

Witness,
Thomas Martin, Jurat
Thomas M. Jones, Jurat

JOSEPH KNOX.

WILL   1843

In the name of God, Amen.

I, Joseph Knox Sen. of the County of Giles & State of Tennessee, being in good health of body and sound mind that it is appointed once for man to die, do make and ordain this my last will and testament in regard to my land that I now own, but no other property at this time, as my other property will be disposed of hereafter.

I give and bequeath to my four sons, John Knox, James Knox, William P.W. Knox and Joseph Knox, all of my land to be equally divided amongst them, and if devided by line, my will is that my son, Joseph Knox, should have the first choice, my tract of land that I bequeath them is situated on the waters of Big Creek in the above named County & State, beginning as follows viz; At the south end corner of Entry No. 445 in the name of Benthall & Gibson, and on the line of William Pea, and Zacharia Tennisen east with the same, one hundred and ten poles to a steak to the line of Jonathan Looney, thence north with the same thirty poles to the south west corner of James Thorns, thence north with his line, one hundred and nine poles to a small dogwood, thence west ninety poles to Benthalls & Gibsons line to a stake, south with the same twenty four poles, thence west with the same fifty poles, thence south with the same one hundred and ninety five poles to the beginning, containing one hundred and sixty three acres.

In testimony whereof I hereunto set my hand and seal this 19th day of August, 1843.

his

JOSEPH X KNOX (Seal)

mark

Attest.
Rufus K. Young, Jurat
T.W. Hewitt, Jurat

GILES COUNTY

LAST WILL AND TESTAMENT
OF
WILLIAM LANE
Dec. 24th A. D. 1839

This loose will was found in the County Court Clerks Office.

Copied by Minnie C. Kellam, Pulaski, Tennessee, September 27th 1938.

State of Tennessee Giles County.

I William Lane, do make and publish this my last will and testement hereby revoking and making void all other wills by me at any time made, First I direct that all my just debts, may be paid as soon after my death as possible out of any money I may die possessed of or may first come into the hands of my Executors, Secondly I give and bequeath unto my beloved wife, Rachael during her natural life or widowhood all the farm on which I now live and all the farm known as the Bunkerhill tract, I likewise bequeath unto her an equal share with my children of all my negro property, all my stock, my household, kitchen furniture, and farming utensals, and an equal share of my interest in the mill and the proceeds there from arrising, Thirdly I bequeath unto each one of children an equal share with my wife of all my negro property & of my stock of farming utensals, and of my household and kitchen furniture and an equal share of my interest in the mill and the proceeds arrising therefrom, Fourthly I bequeath unto my children the tract of land upon which I live and the tract known as the Bunkerhill tract, Lastly I do here by nominate and appoint Thos. I. Lane, & Martin M. Lane, my Executors, in witness whereof I do to this my last will set my hand and seal this 24th day of December A.D. 1839

William Lane. (Seal)

Test
Jacob Jones (Jurat)
Matthew Abernathy, (Jurat)

GILES COUNTY

LAST WILL AND TESTAMENT
OF
ELIZABETH LEE
NOVEMBER 15th 1855

This loose will was found in the County Court Clerks Office.

Copied by Minnie C. Kellam, Pulaski, Tennessee, September 27, 1938.

I Elizabeth Lee, of Giles County Tennessee being of sound mind and memory do ordain and establish this my last will and testament, After my just debts and funeral expenses are paid my will is that my daughter Elizabeth S. Lee, have the use and benefit of my tract of land that I now live on containing about seventy five acres adjoining the lands of Giles A. Reynolds, Albert Buford, and others, during the time she may remain single and unmarried, when my daughter Elizabeth, marries said tract of land is to be sold to the highest bidder by my Executor herein-after appointed and the proceeds of the sale of said tract of land to be equally divided amongst all of my children and the heirs of such as have died (To wit) William W. Lee, John M. Lee, Elizabeth S. Lee, Benjamin J. Lee, Judith Pettus wife of Franklin Pettus, and all the children of Cela P. Brownlow, deceased and said children of said Cela P. are to receive one distributive share or one sixth of the proceeds of the sale of said lands, my will is further that all of my personal property of every description after my death be sold, and the proceeds of such sale be equally devided amongst all of my children, and the children of my daughter Cela P. Brownlow, deceased, being entitled to one share only or one sixth of the proceeds of said sale. My will is and I hereby appoint my son William W. Lee, my Executor of this will, with full power and authority to Execute the same in every particular In witness whereof I have hereunto set my hand and seal (p 2) done and published in the presence of the witnesses whose names are assigned to this will Nov. 15th 1855.

her
Elizabeth x Lee   (Seal)
mark

Witness
Giles A. Reynolds, x
Grandson Wilson,   X

GILES COUNTY

LAST WILL AND TESTAMENT
OF
SUSANNA E. LEE

This loose will was found in the County Court Clerks Office.
Proven May 6th 1844 - Recorded by E. D. Jones, Clerk.

Copied by Minnie C. Kellam, Pulaski, Tennessee, September 27, 1938.

(p 1)   I Susanna E. Lee, do make and pubblish this my last will and
testament hereby revoking and making void all other wills by me at any
time made.   First I direct that my funeral expences and all my debts be
paid as soon after my death as possible out of any money's that I may
die possest of, or may first come into the hands of my Exutox, Secondly
I give and bequeath to my daughter and two Sons, Sarah Lee, John Lee,
and Edward Lee, the tract of land I now live on after deducting out the
amount that John & Edward Lee, has paid in said tract of land, each of
them to have an equal share of my part of said land, & there paying over
their share of my Estate whitch is to be equally devided among all the
heirs of my body, That said Sarah Lee, John Lee, and Edward Lee, is to
have the land valued to them at fourteen hundred dollars, then the amount
taken taken from that amount that John and Edward Lee, has paid.   Thereby
my negro girl Mary and my carrige and horses are to be sold on a twelve
months credit and the proceds to go equal to the heirs of my daughter
Mary and to my daughter Frances Franklin, (p 2) and to my daughter
Harriett Robston, & to my daughter Martha Ann Nix, My will is that the
above named Sarah Lee, & John Lee, & Edward Lee, shall not be Pestered
for the amount that they have to pay the other heirs is there should be
anything going to them, untill they have time to make the amount, lastly
I do hereby nominate and appoint John Robetson, & John Lee, my executors
in witness whereof I do to this my will set my hand and seal this the
10th day of May A.D. in year of our Lord 1842

                                             her
                              Susanna E.   x Lee   (Seal)
                                            mark

Signed sealed and published in our presants and we have subscribed our
names hereto in the presants of the Testator this the 10th day of
May 1842

A. K. Moore (Jurat)
W. R. Davis
W. R. J. Husbands, (Jurat)

ELIZABETH LESTER

WILL 1830

In the name of God, Amen.

I, Elizabeth Lester in the County of Giles, in the State of Tennessee being of sound mind but of advanced age and feeble in body do make and ordain this my last will and testament.

First, I resign my body to the grave and my soul to Almighty God, who gave it.

Secondly, I desire to be decently intered and my just debts and funeral expences paid.

Thirdly, I give and bequeath all my Estate, goods and chattels to my son, German Lester, and everything that I may die possessed of except such part thereof as I only had a life Estate in, and which belonged to my deceased husbands estate, Henry Lester and by him otherwise disposed of in his last will and testament. I have been induced thus to dispose of my small effects because many of the articles now in my possession were given to me by my son, German Lester and because at his own request his father excluded him from any share of his effects in his will and the share that he would have otherwise received was of course divided amongst the other Legatees.

Fourthly, I hereby appoint my son, German Lester, sole executor of this my last will and testament.

Witness my hand and seal this 4th day of January 1830.

her
ELIZABETH X LESTER
mark

Witness,
John Shall
Ann X Evans
    her
    mark
Fountain Lester

GILES COUNTY

LAST WILL AND TESTAMENT
OF
JAMES LESTER
Nov. A. D. 1840

This loose will was found in the County Court Clerks Office.

Copied by Minnie C. Kellam, Pulaski, Tennessee, September 27th 1938.

I James Lester, of the county of Giles and state of Tennessee, being of sound mind and memory but in bad health, and not knowing when I may be called to another mode of ixantance and knowing after the expiration of this year that my family will be without a home, and being anctious that they should have one provided in time to move to by Christmas next, I doe hereby make this my last will and testament hereby appoint my wife as Executrix to my will without giving security, my will further is that my wife dispose of such part of my stock of horses, cows, and hogs and notes due me, or which may become due in the best way she can, so as to pay off all my just debts, and should there not be money enough left to purchase a comfortable home for the family then & in that case to sell such of my Negroes as she may think proper to get such home, my will further is that she keep and raise my children and as they come of age give to each child a proportionate share of negroes & stock, & money, my will further is that my wife shall and keep possession of the land to be bought, during her life or widowhood to raise my children on without charge, but should she marry, my will is that she have a childs part of my property both real and personal, in testemony whereof I hereunto (p 2) set my hand and seal, this 20th October 1840.

(Seal)

John Cheatham
James Flaut.

69

SALLY LINDSEY.

WILL 1841

In the name of God, Amen.

I, Sally Lindsey, being sound in mind but weak in body from age, knowing the uncertainity of life and certainity of death do make and ordain this my last will and testament, towit; I give to my grandchildren, Sarah T. Moore, Martha Ann Moore, Robert Moore, & James McCord Moore, all my negroes, and money to be kept together or hired out as my son in law Benjamin Carter may think best, as it is my wish that he take possession of the same and manage it for them, and also out od the proceeds of the same viz; the hire and interest, it is my will that my daughter Lucinda A. Moore, have a support in common with her children, but should she at any time ever live with her husband, William H. Moore, or become so situated by divorce or otherwise that she could marry again and should she do so in either event it is my will that she no longer receive any support as above named, but should she continue to live in her present situation It is my will that the property continued together untill James McCord Moore, becomes twenty one years old, at which time it is my wish that the property be equally divided between my four grandchildren above named. And then Lucinda A. Moores support to ceade as her children will then be her natural protectors; I also give to my daughters, Mary Kearney, Martha Andrews, Elizabeth Carter & Mariah Coe, one bed each (Elizabeth & Martha has received theirs) I have one at Doct. Carters. and one at my sons, John Lindseys, these are the two I design for my daughters, Mary & Mariah.

In witness whereof, I hereunto set my hand and seal this 3rd day of August, 1838.

SARAH LINDSEY (Seal)

In preasance of
Guston Kearney
Jno. G. Andrews

This day was produced in open court the foregoing will which was proven according to law by Guston Kearney, one of the subscribing witnesses & it is therefore admitted to probate and record in this court May 24th 1841.

William S. Bailey, Judge of Probate.

The State of Mississippi, Madison County Probate Court, May term 1841.

Personally appeared before me William S. Bailey, Judge of the Probate Court in & for said County & State, Guston Kearney, one of the subscribing witnesses to the within will, who being duly sworn deposed & said state he saw Sarah Lindsey the testatrix sign and seal said will, that he signed the same as a testing witness in her presence and at her request & in the presence of John G. Andrews, the other subscribing witness who also signed the same in the presence & at the request of the said testratrix on the day of the date of the exeoution of said will towit, On the 3rd day of August 1838, and also that said testratrix was at the time of executing said/of sound mind and disposing memory.

GUSTON KEARNEY

Sworn to & subscribed in open court this 24th day of May A.D. 1841
Williss Pass, Judge of Probate.

Sally Lindsey Will
Page 2

The foregoing certificate of affidavit was improperly written & this paper pasted on in order to amend & the masures in said affidavit were made by me. Given under my hand & seal 24th May 1841.

WILLIS BAILEY (Seal)
Judge &.

GILES COUNTY

LAST WILL AND TESTAMENT
OF
RICHARD LIPSCOMB
JULY 4, 1832

This loose will was found in the County Court Clerks Office.

Copied by Minnie C. Kellam, Pulaski, Tennessee, Sept. 27, 1938.

I Richard Lipscomb, of Charlotte County make these my last will
and testament. I bequeath to my children Robert K. Lipscomb,
Mary E. Lipscomb, and Ambrose Lipscomb equal division of my Estate
after my just debts are paid, My wife Polly Lipscomb is to live of my
estate, during her natural life or widowhood, I wish my estate to keep
together untill my Son Ambrose is 21 years old, and he is to have
education sufficient to do his business, to read, write & cypher, and
when Ambrose is 21 years old, my estate may be divided equally between
my - Robert K. Lipscomb, Mary E. Lipscomb & Ambrose Lipscomb, if they
choose, If not they may live with their mother as heretofore, my wife
Polly Lipscomb and her son Robert K. Lipscomb, is to have the management
of my estate and make a support for the family, they may put hands
on my land in Macklenburg County and make what they can, If there is
more made than supports the family at either place all must have their
part. No waste is to be committed on the estate, if Robert K. Lipscomb,
Mary E. Lipscomb, or Ambrose Lipscomb, die without heirs lawful begotten
their part of my estate they have to return into my estate again
Witness my hand and seal July 4th 1832

                              Richard Lipscomb, (Seal)

I Polly Lipscomb sanction the above will,
                    Polly Lipscomb,   (Seal)

Attest
Wm. Cook
Mary B. Brooks
Saluda Britt
Mildred H. Lewis
George C. Robey
Leroy J. Farmer

      At a court held for Charlott County March 4th 1839 this last will
and testament of Richard Lipscomb dec'd was presented in court, and the
same was proven by the oaths of George C. Robey, and Leroy J. Farmer, two
of the subscribing witnesses to be the last will and testament of the said
Richard Lipscomb, dec'd. and ordered to be recorded and on the motion of
Robert K. Lipscomb, (p 2) who made oath thereto according to law, And
together with Andrew Middleton, John Middleton, John W. Deshazer,
Cain J. Gaines, John Osborn, and John Garnett, his securities entered into

and acknowledged bond in the penalty of twenty five thousand dollars, conditioned as the law requires, certificate is granted him for obtaining letters of administration of the Estate of the said Richard K. Lipscomb, dec'd. in due form, with the said will annexed,

    Teste Winslow Robinson, Clk

Copy The Winslow Robinson, Clk.

State of Virginia, Charlotte County

    I Winslow Robinson, Clerk of the County Court of Charlotte in the State of Virginia, do hereby certify that the foregoing is a copy of the will of Richard Lipscomb decd. as entered of word in my office.

    In testimony whereof I have hereto set my hand and a office no Seal of my office this 22nd day of February 1845

                Winslow Robinson, C. C. (Seal)

ALEXANDER LOCK.

WILL 1821

In the name of God, Amen.

I, Alexander Lock, of the County of Giles and State of Tennessee, do make this my last will and testament.

First, It is my will for all my land in Bedford County and State aforesaid to be sold for to pay my just debts and if there should be a residue remaining, then the same to be equally divided between my wife, Ann Lock, my daughter Sally Watson and my two sons George W. Lock & John B. Lock.

It is my desire for my wife, Ann Lock to have her share of one bed & furniture to her own use, and dispose of it at her death as she may think proper.

I give and bequeath to my son, George W. Lock one other bed and furniture.

I leave to my son, John B. Lock one other bed and furniture.

I will to my wife Ann Lock, my negro boy Sam, as long as she lives single, also my negro girl Jane to her and her heirs forever to dispose of at her death, the said negro Jane, as she may think proper.

I will to my son George W. Lock, my negro boy, Parker and one bay mare to him and his heirs forever.

I will and bequeath to my son, John B. Lock my negro girl Hannah and one two year old filly to him and his heirs forever.

It is my desire that my negroes and my stock may remian on my plantation as long as my wife and two sons may live together.

I will my plantation and my rights in the mills that are on the plantation, equally to my wife, Ann Lock and John B. Lock, and at the death of my wife, Ann Lock the said plantation to fall to my two sons and their heirs forever.

I bequeath to my daughter Sally Watson, one fourth part of all my lands on the Forked Deer & Obion rivers to her and her heirs forever and the remaining three fourths to my wife, Ann Lock and my two sons, George W. Lock and John B. Lock, to them and their heirs forever.

It is my will and desire that all of my stock, my household and kitchen furniture and every other spetious of property that I have not willed and bequeathed to go equal to my wife, Ann Lock and my two sons George W. Lock and John B. Lock and their heirs forever. In witness whereof I have hereunto set my hand and affixed my seal this 28th day of February in the year of our Lord one thousand eight hundred and twenty one.

ALEXANDER LOCK (Seal)

Signed, sealed and delivered
by the testators as his last
will and testament, in the
presence of us.
Jno. S. Brandon
Robert Reed
Charles Myers, Junior
    I also do appoint my son, George W. Lock, to execute my will provided

Alexander Look Will
Page 2

he becomes of mature age before my death. If he does not become of mature age before my death, then and in that case, I do appoint my true and tried friend, Richard Brandon, my Executor.
February 28th 1821

    Asigned, Alexr. Look.

GILES COUNTY

WILL OF
ABNER LOCKE
FEBRUARY 23, 1821

This loose will was found in the County Court Clerks Office.

Copied by Minnie C. Kellam, Pulaski, Tennessee, Sept. 27, 1938.

In the name of God Amen

I Abander Lock of the County of Giles and State of Tennessee, do make this my last will and testament, first it is my will for all my land in Bedford County, and state aforesaid to be sold for to pay my just debts and if there should be a besides remaining then the sum to be equally divided between my wife Ann Locke, my daughter Sallie Watson, and my two sons George W. Locke, and John B. Locke, It is my desire for my wife Ann Locke, to have her choice of one bed and furniture to her own proper use and dispose of it at her death as she may think proper, I give and bequeath to my son George W. Locke, one other bed and furniture, I leave to my son John B. Lock, one other bed and furniture I will to my wife Ann Locke, my negro boy Sam as long as she lives single also my negro girl Jane, to her and to her heirs for ever to dispose of at her death the said negro Jane as she may think proper. I will to my son George W. Locke, my negro (p 2) Boy Parker, and one Bay mare to him and his heirs forever. I will and bequeath to my son John B. Locke, my negro girl Hannah, and one two year old filly to him and his heirs forever. It is my desire that my negroes and my stock may remain on my plantation as long as my wife and two sons may live together I will my plantation and my Right in the Mills, that are on the plantations, Equally to my wife Ann Locke, and my two sons George W. Lock & John B. Locke, and at the death of my wife Ann Locke, the said plantation to fall to my two sons and their heirs forever.

I bequeath to my daughter Sallie Watson, one fourth part of all my lands on the forked Deer, and Obion River, to her and her heirs forever and the remaining three fourts to my wife Ann Locke, and my two sons, George W. Locke and John B. Locke, to them and their heirs forever - It is my will and my desire that all of my (p 3) stock my household and kitchen furniture and all other property that I have not willed and bequeathed to go equally to my wife Ann Locke, and my two sons George W. Locke, and John B. Locke, and their heirs forever.

In witness whereof I have set my hand and afixed my seal this the 28th day of February in the year of our Lord one thousand eight hundred and twenty one

Abn Locke, (Seal)

Signed sealed and declaired by the testators as his last will and testament in the presence of us.

John S. Brandon,
Robert Reed,
Charles Myers, Jr.

I also do appoint my son George W. Locke, to execute my will provided he becomes of mature age before my death, if he does not become of mature age before my death then and in that case I do appoint my true and trusty friend Richard Brandon my Executor.

February 28th 1821   Signed

Abn Locke.

GILES COUNTY

LAST WILL AND TESTAMENT
OF
STEPHEN LOYD
APRIL 11, 1831

This loose will was found in the County Court Clerks Office.

Copied by Minnie C. Kellam, Pulaski, Tennessee, September 27, 1938.

In the name of God Amen
        I, Stephen Loyd of the County of Giles and state of Tennessee,
being of sound mind and disposing memory do make and ordain this my
last will and testement in the manner and form that followeth
(To wit) Item 1st. After all my just debts are paid I will & bequeath
to my beloved wife Elizabeth, one negro girl Fatha, one negro girl
Hannah, one negro girl Lucy, one negro boy Nicholas, all my household
and kitchen furniture. All my stock of horses, cattle, sheep, & hogs
my tract of land containing 253 acres together with all my plantation
tools, poultry &c to have and to hold during her widowhood, should she
marry, I wish an equal division of all my property to be made among my
children, Susan, William, Martha, James, Sally, John, Eliza, Elizabeth,
& Catharine. In consequence of affection, I wish my son James to have
one hundred dollars more than an equal proportion, When William arrives
at twenty one years of age he will be entitled to a young bay horse
called Doctor, I nominate Stephen Hightower & Marshall Boyce, as
executors to this my last will and testement, hereby revoking and disannulling all others by me made, whereof I hereunto (p 2) set my hand
and seal this the second of September one thousand and eight hundred and
twenty six, signed sealed and delivered in presence of us

                                        his
                            Stephen x Loyd (Seal)
                                       mark

Codicil
James Maegowan
Wm. P. Booth

In addition to what is contained in the above will, I also wish my two
younger children Stephen Coleman, and Alexander Green, to be considered
as equally entitled to as much as others of the other above named heirs,
James and William Excepted but this codicil in no otherwise to affect any
other part or provision before made in witness, I have again set my hand
and seal this 11th day of April 1831

                                        his
                            Stephen x Loyd
                                       mark

Test
Robert McLaurine
Henry Loyd

SUSAN M. LOYD

WILL 1846

In the name of God, Amen.

I, Susan M. Loyd, being infirm in body but sound of mind, and memory, thanks be to God for the same, and collecting to mind that it is appointed unto to man once to die, I do hereby make and constitute this to be my last will and testament (that is to say) I resign my body to its mother earth to be buried in a decent manner and recommend my soul to God who gave it, then I decree all my just debts and funeral expences paid and afterward my will is that all of my property, (viz) one negro woman named Lucy and her increase if any, one bed, bedstead and bed clothes, cupboard ware, and one side saddle, to belong to my sister, Martha A. Grubbs, during her natural life and then to go to the heirs of her body forever.

I do hereby constitute and appoint Nicholas Grubbs, husband of the aforesaid Martha A. Grubbs, the sole Executor of this, my last will and testament and authorize him to pay my debts and funeral expences aforesaid in any way that may seem best with him.

In testimony whereof I have hereunto set my hand and seal the 24th day of June in the year of our Lord, 1846.

SUSAN M. LOYD (Seal)

Testim
Willeford x
J. Mays x

JAMES R. LUKER

WILL 1835

In the name of God, Amen.

I, James R. Luker, being weak in body, but of sound and perfect mind
and memory, blessed be Almighty God for the same, do make and publish
this my last will and testament in manner and form following, that is to
say, first that all my just debts to be paid.

Secondly, I give and bequeath unto my beloved wife, Elizabeth Luker
two hundred and thirteen acres of land, lying and being in the County of
Giles and State of Tennessee on the waters of Richland Creek. I also
give her all my personal property her lifetime or widowhood, if she should
marry the Estate to be sold as the law directs and the money to be equally
divided with all my children towit; Eldagentia Luker and John Brasil
Luker and James Richmond Luker and Charity Luker and Joseph Luker and
Rivaries McCoy Luker and George Washington Luker, and Jerome Pillow Luker,
and as they become of age, that is if she thinks proper to give them some-
thing that she should take account of it that all should be made equal
of this my last will and testament, hereby revoking all former wills by
me made. In witness whereof I have hereunto set my hand and seal this
third day of June in the year of our Lord, 1835.

J.R. LUKER (Seal)

Test
John Young, Senior
John R. Luker.

GEORGE OLIVER

WILL 1833

In the name of God, Amen.

I, George Oliver, in sound mind and memory do make this my last will and testament, viz, After all my lawful debts are paid and I myself decently buried, I will and bequeath to my son, Annanias Oliver, one tract of land containing thirty acres on the waters of Buchanan Creek, adjoining my home tract, also his own land (S. Oliver's).

2nd. I will and bequeath to my loving wife, Ann Oliver, my tract of land which I now live on, during her lifetime, also negro man Frank, and negro woman, Aimy, and child Judy, with all necessary stock of horses, cows, hogs, sheep, with all the farming utinseals and every other thing pertaing to my property for her use during her life and for the benefit of the family while they stay together.

3rd. I will and bequeath to my daughter, Charlotte C. Oliver, negro girl, Judy, and horse worth seventy dollars and saddle and bridle, bed, bedstead, furniture and one bureau.

4th. I will and bequeath to my daughter, Esther Croft and her children fifty dollars in money.

5th. I will and bequeath to my neice Martha Tarkington, one bed, bedstead and furniture and one horse worth fifty dollars, one saddle & bridle.

6th. I will and bequeath to my grandson George C. Oliver, fifty dollars or a horse worth that ammount.

7th. I will and bequeath to my grand daughter, Malinda M. Oliver, fifty dollars, or a horse worth that sum.

8th. I will and bequeath to my son, William H. Oliver, the tract of land that I now live on containing two hundred and sixty acres, more or less, one horse worth eighty dollars, one saddle and bridle, one bed, bedstead and furniture & one chest.

9th. After the death of my wife, Ann Oliver, all the residue of my property not designated in my testament is to be equally divided between my four surviving children, Annanias Oliver, Charlotte C. Oliver, William H. Oliver & Esther Croft.

10th. I appoint my friend, Robert Oliver Esq. to be my guardian for my daughter, Esther and her children over the property that I have bequeathed to them.

11th. I appoint my two sons, Annanias and William H. Oliver to be Executors to my last will and testament, this 22nd. day of December, A.D. 1833. Signed and acknowledged in the presence of witnesses.

                                        his
                            GEORGE   X   OLIVER (Seal)
                                        mark

William Young, Jurat
Holley Harwell, Jurat

THOMAS ORR

WILL 1853

Know all men by these presents that I, Thomas Orr, of the County of Giles and State of Tennessee, being of sound mind and memory, do make the following disposition of my property as my last will & testament, viz;

1st. For the love I bear to the Church of Jesus Christ, by whose grace I hope to be saved & in consideration of especial anxiety for the prosperity of the Bear Creek Congregation of the Cumberland Presbyterian church, established in the southwestern corner of Marshall County & State of Tennessee, I do give and bequeath to James Orr, Wm. H. Pickens, James B. Lowery, Wm. Calvert & Ashley Moore, Ruling Elders in said congregation & their successors in office forever, the sum of three thousand dollars to be kept by them at lawful interest & the interest appropriated annually to the support of the pastor of said Bear Creek Church, provided always that said church shall raise annually a sum equal at least to said annual interest, for the same purpose, otherwise at the end of each year, succeeding each failure to comply with this proviso, said bench of Elders shall pay over the interest of said fund for that year to the Cumberland Presbyterian Board of Foriegn and Domestic Missions, for carrying on their work, or provided, secondly, a Pastor is employed for any one year for a salary less than double the annual interest of said fund, then half of the salary shall be paid out of said interest & the remainder shall be paid over to the Board of Missions, as above, said Bench of Elders shall be held accountable for the duties herein assigned them. To the Board of Trustees of Cumberland Presbyterian Church, 2nd. Tender the firm conviction that education as a handmaid of religion is a great blessing to the church of Jesus Christ & mankind at large. I give and bequeath to the Board of Trustees of Cumberland University, nine hundred dollars with which added to a donation of one hundred dollars for which they now hold my note.

I hereby endow a scholarship in said Institution the benefit of which shall first redound to my nephew, David A. Lowery & forever afterwards to canidates for the Holy Ministry under the care of the Elk Presbytery of the Cumberland Presbyterian Church.

3rd. For the love and affection I have for my beloved brother and sisters, James Orr, Polly Kerr & Elizabeth Lowery, I give and bequeath to them the balance of entire Estate to be equally divided between them, either by a division or sale of the property of James B. Lowery by his paying three hundred & thirty dollars into the funds for distribution according to contract when said slave was purchased.

4th. And finally It is my will & I hereby appoint James Orr, John Kerr & James B. Lowery, the Executors of this my last will and testament.

In witness whereof, I hereunto sign my name & affix my seal on the day and date first written.

THOMAS ORR (Seal)

Signed and sealed in our presence
on the day & date above stated.
Peter R. Jones, Jurat
Thos. J. Farmer, Jurat

NETY J. PAGE

WILL 1860

State of Tennessee, Giles County.

In the name of God, Amen.

I, Nety J. Page, being of sound and disposing mind and memory and considering the uncertainity of this mortal life, do make and declair this my last will and testament in manner and form following;

First I give and bequeath and devise to my three children, Isaac Washington, Robert Cobal and Mary Eliza, my tract of land on which we now live, containing by estimation two hundred and twenty five acres or thereabout, the said land is not yet paid for, my will is that it be paid for as follows; My first to the Clerk and Master to be paid off out of the proceeds of a note, I hold on John J. Morris, for about two hundred & thirty dollars, and a note on David H. Hannah & John H. Rhea for about eighty eight dollars. My second note to the Clerk and Master to be paid out of the produce of my three mare's and if the colts of the mares are not sufficient, I want one or more of the mares sold to make the last payment, and I wish my beloved husband to live appon and enjoy the said land for the purpose of raising my children and when the youngest child becomes of lawful age, then I wish it sold or divided equally between the three children. I wish any and all other things kept in the family for the purpose of raising & schooling the children. I hereby appoint my friend, Hugh Yokley, my Executor of this my last will and testament.

Witness my hand and seal this April 1st. 1860

her

NETY J. X PAGE (Seal)

mark

Test.

J.J. Morris, x

Joshua Morris x

JAMES PAISLEY.

WILL 1844

I, James Paisley do make this my last will and testament hereby revoking and making void all wills by me made at any time.

First, I direct that mt funeral expences and all my debts be paid as
soon as possible, as I have given to my three sons, John A. Paisley,
James D. Paisley and Wm. R.D. Paisley, their part in land & the balance
of my land I give to my beloved wife, Hannah Paisley, during her life,
then to belong to my daughters, Jane Paisley, Nancy Paisley, Elioner
Paisley, and Mary Ann Paisley. If they remain single, but if either of
them should marry they with my daughters, Hannah M. Jones and Francis
Jones, must get as near as possible the amount of property, we gave Anne
Kerr. I also leave for the use of my beloved wife and family, all my
stock of every kind, also my wagon and farming utinsils to the use and
benefit of the plantation, also all my household & kitchen furniture, to
my wife and above nameddaughter that live with her. I also give the use
of the meeting house and campground to the use of Cumberland Presbyterian
Church so long as there remains a society at that place, but if disolved
to return back to the use of my family.

Lastly, I do hereby nominate and appoint John A. Paisley and James
D. Paisley, my Executors, to this my last will and testament. Whereof I
set my hand and seal this 25th day of March 1844.

JAMES PAISLEY (Seal)

In presence of
James D. Paisley, Jurat
Wm. R.D. Paisley, Jurat

EPHRIAM PARHAM

WILL 1818

In the name of God, Amen.

I, Ephriam Parham, of Giles County and State of Tennessee, do ordain this my last will and testament in manner and form as follows; towit;

To my daughter, Rebeccah Pressgee, I give one negro woman, by the name of Silvey, a negro man by the name of Jesse, also one negro boy by the name of Peter, who is now in her possession to her and her heirs forever.

To my daughter, Nancy Hamilton, I give one negro man by the name of Burwell, to her and her heirs forever.

To my son, Peterson G. Parham, I give one negro boy, by the name of Isham, to him and his heirs forever.

To my wife Polly Parham, Thomas Parham, Demasene Parham, Permelia Parham and Maude Parham, I give all the rest and residue of my Estate, after my just debts are paid.

I also wish Doctor John Camp to serve as an Administrator to the above.

EPHRIAM PARHAM (Seal)

Also,
Signed, sealed and delivered
in our presence.
John Camp
Thos. Harwood

JEREMIAH PARKER

WILL 1840

My last Will and Testament.
In the name of God, Amen.

I, Jeremiah Parker of the County of Giles and State of Tennessee, being sick and weak of body, but of a perfect mind and memory, thanks be to God Almighty, Calling to mind the the immortality of my body, knowing it is appointed for all men once to die, do make this my last will and testament that is to say, principally & first of all, I recommend my soul into the hands of Almighty God, that gave it & my body to the earth to be buried in decency at the discretion of my friends, nothing doubting at the general Ressurection, I shall receive the same again by the power of God. And as touching things of a worldly nature that God has bestowed on me of his great goodness for this life, I give and dispose in the following manner.

After my just debts are paid, I give and bequeath unto my beloved wife, Milly Parker & Lilah Parker, my daughter, the farm which they now live on, with all of its profits ariving from it for their support & comforts, also my rone mare & colt & filey. my horse, bridle, and saddle two of the best of my cows and calves, ten head of my best hogs to fatten for this fall, 1840 & ten of my best shotes for the next fall 1841, two of the choicest of my sow and pigs in my flock of hogs & all my household and kitchen furniture, except one bed & furniture.

I give and bequeath to my grand daughter Mary Brown when she needs it & twenty dollars in cash to help her take care of her grandmother till she marries, also the farming tools with the farm for their use and comfort so long as my wife lives & my daughter Lilah lives single & after her mother's death if she should marry, in that case I give and bequeath to her my daughter, Lilah Parker, my young filie horse, bridle and saddle, two choice cows and calves, two sows & pigs, six killing hogs for meat next fall, 1840 & ten shotes, two beds & furniture of her own choice, one cupboard, one small table, one sugar chest & one hundred dollars in cash forever, and all the rest of my real and personal property to be sold & equally divided between my children that is to say, my son, Zachariah Parker, my daughter, Polly McConnell, my daughter Lilah Parker, my son, John Parker, Linnie Brown, my daughter, her part of my estate to be divided between her five children, Lindy, Camron, Sealy Gaines, John Brown, Peggy Brown, Mary G. Brown, equally I say again that all my surplus property not mentioned in my will to be sold & equally divided among the legatees according to my request to them and their offsprings, forever.

Rattifying this and no other to be my last will and testament, whereof I have hereunto set my hand and affixed my seal this day of ----- 1840.

JEREMIAH PARKER (Seal)

Interlined before signed, signed & delivered by me, Jeremiah Parker, as my last will and Testament in the presence of us, Tests.
x x
It is my will that Zacheriah Parker & John Parker should execute my will between all the legatees according to my will truly.

JEREMIAH PARKER

JOHN PATRICK SR.

WILL 1827

State of Tennessee)
Giles County   )   In the name of God, Amen.

I, John Patrick, Sr. being in my propper mind and memory and calling
to mind the mortality of my body, knowing that it is appointed for all men
once to die, I do make and ordain this my last will & Testament in manner
an form following, (Viz)

First, of all I recommend my sole into the hand of God, who gave it
and my body to the dust to be decently buried by my hereafter named Executors, and as touching my worldly Estate, wherewith it hath pleased God
to bless me. I give and bequeath as follows (Viz)

1st. It is my desire that all my just debts should be paid by
Executors out of my Estate.

2nd. I give and bequeath to my dear daughter in law, Katy Patrick
the sum of five dollars .

3rd. To my dear son in law, Wm. Stephenson, five dollars.

4th. To my dear son, John Patrick, five dollars

5th. To my dear son inlaw Joseph Armour, five dollars.

6th. To my dear daughter, Mary Tuttle, five dollars.

7th. To my dear son, Ephriam Patrick, five dollars.

8th. To my dear daughter, Hannah Montgomery five dollars

9th. To my dear son, Samuel Patrick, five dollars.

The balance of my estate real and personal I give and bequeath to Jane C.
Patrick & Ephriam M. Patrick, children of my son, Ephriam Patrick, after
my death to be equally divided between them.

And I do hereby ordain, constitute and appoint my beloved friends,
Ephriam Patrick & Chas. M. Patrick, my lawful and able Executors to this
my last will & Testament and all others made by me to be null and void to
all intents and purposes. In witness, whereof I have hereunto set my
hand and seal this 4th. day of February 1827.

                                        JOHN PATRICK (Seal)

Tests.
John M. Patrick
Margaret K. Patrick

JOHN PAUL
WILL 1823

State of Tennessee)
Giles County)
February 4th 1823)   In the name of God, Amen.

I, John Paul of State of Tennessee and County aforesaid, being weakly
in body, but in perfect mind and memory (thanks be to God for his unspeak-
able mercies) but calling to mind the mortality of my body & knowing that
it is appointed unto all men once to die, I therefore think proper in this
manner & at this time to dispose of what little worldly property, it has
pleased God to bless me with, That is to say,
First, of all I ordain & appoint my beloved wife, Sally & Harrison Burgess
as my sole Executors & as touching my property, I leave & bequeath, that
is to say first of all I commend my soul into the hands of God, who gave
it & my body to the dust, to be buried in a decent Christain manner at the
direction of my Executors, nothing doubting that at the general Resurrection I shall receive the same again by the power of Almighty God & in the
next place I leave unto my brother David Paul, ten shillings & to my
sister, Elizabeth, ten shillings & to my brother, William Paul I leave
ten shillings & also my sister Susanna I leave ten shillings & to my sister Hannah I leave ten shillings, & to my brother Samuel Paul I leave ten
shillings, also to my brother, Daniel I leave ten shillings.

All the rest of my property consisting of lands, horses, cattle,
farming utensils & household furniture I leave and bequeath to my beloved
wife Sally, for her use and behalf during her life or widowhood, I make
my brother in law, Harrison Burgess my sole heir of all the remaining property belonging to my estate, to use and dispose of as he may think proper. And I do hereby utterly & solemnly revoke & disallow all other wills
& testaments, made by me & firmly avow this to be my last will & testament
In confirmation whereof I have hereunto set my hand and affixed my seal,
the day and date above.

                                            her
                                 JOHN   PAUL (Seal)
                                            mark

Signed, sealed & delivered
in presence of Samuel D. Lawson, Jurat
John Wilson
Harrison   X   Burgess
         his
         mark

JAMES M. PAXTON

WILL 1818

In the name of God, Amen.

I bequeath my Estate to my wife and child after all my just debts
are paid, so long as she remains my widow, but if she should marry, she
is to have the amount of what she had when we were married, the rest to
go to my daughter. My wife and brother, Thompson Paxton to be Executor
and Executrix this 19th of August, 1818.

JAMES M. PAXTON, (Seal)

Nathaniel Young, Jurat
Hugh Young, Jurat
Rosanna Davidson, Jurat

MATTHIAS PETTY

WILL 1832

In the name of God, Amen.

I, Matthias Petty, being in bad health, but of sound mind, do make
this my last will and testament, in manner and form following:

First, I resign my soul to Almighty God, and my body I commit to
the earth to be buried at the discretion of my Executor & Executrix,
who will be hereafter named.

First, I bequeath and give to my dear wife, Elizabeth, all my real
and personal Estate during her life or widowhood and at her death to be
equally divided amongst my beloved children, (Viz) Elizabeth, William,
Thompson, Julian, Matthias, Daniel and Robert James and a proportionable
part of two tracts of my whole Estate to be paid to the above named
children as they become of age or marry, and in the event that my wife
should marry then she to have the one third part of all my Estate, and at
her death to be equally divided with the above named children and the two
thirds as they become of age or marry as above named and for doing and
executing the same I do appoint George Malone, Sr. and my wife Executor
& Executrix of this my last will and testament.

In testimony whereof I have hereunto set my hand and seal this 20th
day of July 1832.

MATTHIAS PETTY (Seal)

Test,
J.E. Tomlinson
John Gordon

REESE PORTER

WILL 1817

In the name of God, Amen

I, Reese Porter of Giles County and State of Tennessee, being weak in
body, but of perfect mind and sound memory & calling to mind the certainity of death & the uncertainity of the time it may happen, do make and &
ordain this as my last will & testament, revoking & hereby disannuling
all former wills & testaments by me hereafter made; In the first place
I give and command my soul to Almighty God who gave it, and my body to
the dust, hoping for the resurrection of the dead, and as touching such
worldly Estate wherewith it has pleased God to bless me with in this life.
I give and dispose of in the following manner towit;
In the first place, I give and bequeath to my son, William Porter, 5
dollars, and have conveyed to his children, Nimrod Porter, Reese Porter,
Hugh Porter, John Porter & Jane B. Porter, two hundred and eighty one
acres of land, the western end of a tract of five hundred and forty acres
granted to me by the State of North Carolina, by Grant no. ——— & lying
on little Tom Bigby creek, expressed in the face of said deed that the
said William have liberty to cultivate fifty acres of said tract, during
his life. It is expressly my will and was my intention in making said
deed to the said Nimrod Porter, Reese, Hugh, John, & Jane, that they would
at all times keep the said William in peaceable possession of the above
named fifty acres for his support during his life and during the life of
his wife, Jane.
I likewise did convey by deed to my son, Joseph B. Porter, all the
balance of said tract of five hundred and forty acres of land & to my son
John Porter, three hundred and ten acres. part of a tract of two thousand
acres lying on Richland Creek, Giles County, to the heirs of Reese Porter,
Deceased, a lot in said two thousand acre tract as expressed in said deed
to David W. Porter, likewise a lot in said two thousand acre tract as expressed in said deed.
To James B. Porter, three hundred and twenty seven acres of said two
thousand acre tract as expressed in said conveyance & to Thomas C. Porter
& Jane B. Porter, I will and bequeath the tract of land I now live on
containing two hundred and forty acres, being a lot of said two thousand
acre tract, in the following manner. The said Thomas is entitaled to the
value of seventy three acres, the south end of the lot conveyed to said
Jane B. of said tract to be equally divided between them, seventy three
acres more than one equal half my plantation in Davidson County, whereon
I formerly lived. I wish my Executors to sell and the proceeds of said
sale to be equally divided amongst my sons, William, Joseph, John, David,
James & Thomas and the heirs of my son, Reese in right of their father,
subject to a deduction of fifty dollars, which sum I heretofore let him
have, and further that the Administrators of said Estate pay a note given
by me to G.W. Campbell, for fifty dollars & such interest as may have
accrued thereon, as the said Reese in his lifetime promised to do and
whereas there yet remains due & sum not yet determined to Robert Worley
for his locating fees for the land above described & conveyed and the
express terms on which conveyances & devises were made were that my
jural heirs should pay their respective shares of such sum (if any be
adjudged) as may be yet due agreeable to their respective shares of said

land. I give and bequeath to my grand daughter Jane B. Porter, five dollars, together with a bed & curtains I have already given her.

I give and bequeath to my beloved wife, Lucy Porter, one horse called Dick, one cow, her choice of my stock, three sheep, three or four breeding sows, all her choice, one hundred bushels of corn, a sufficient quantity of wheat & meat to support her one year, with liberty to live in my dwelling house one year, if she should thinkproper and should she wish to remain I recommend to my sons to whom my plantation is divised to suffer her to remain in possession of a part of my house with them, and to pay her fifty dollars out of the money now on hand together with all her own property now in my possession.

I give and bequeath to my sons, James B. Porter & Thos. C. Porter, my negro man Aaron & woman Frances, my stock of horses, cattle, sheep, & hogs my farming tools & household furniture not otherwise disposed of with the kitchen furniture, likewise a still and all my money now in hand, note book, accounts &. and rifle gun.

I give and bequeath to my son, William Porter a land warrent for ninety five acres now in the hands of Joseph B. Porter.

I do by these present nominate & appoint my sons, John Porter, James B. Porter & Thomas C. Porter, Executors of this my last will & testament and do not require that they give security for the same, signed sealed & declared by the said Reese Porter as my last will and testament, this 27th of September 1817 in the presence of us & we in the presence of each other.

                                                    REESE PORTER (Seal)

John B. Brandon
John M. Hobson
John M. Duff
(Handwriting proven Nov. 1822)

Lauson Hobson deposeth. I was well acquainted with John M. Hobson one of the subscribing witnesses to the will of Reese Porter, deceased, late of Giles County, and I am well acquainted with his handwriting. I believe that the signature of said John M. Hobson to said will annexed as a witness is his own proper handwriting. And I do believe that said John M. Hobson is dead, having been absent better than twelve months, and also from reports and circumstances I have been particular in my inquiries after said John M. Hobson, he being my son. Whereupon the court considers the will of Reese Porter as being fully proven & order the same to be certified for registration.
Recorded the above & issued letters of Testamony without Executors, giving security as John Willis directed.

JAMES PULLEY

WILL 1837

I, James Pulley, of the County of Giles and State of Tennessee, being of sound mind and memory, do make this my last will and Testament.

Item 1st. It is my will and desire, in the first place after my decease, that my debts be paid out of any money on hand or that may arise from the sale of my Estate.

Item 2nd. I leave my beloved wife, my land, household and kitchen furniture during her life or widowhood. In the event of her marrying again, or at her death, it is my desire that it be equally divided among my children or the heirs of their body..

Item 3rd. I leave my wife, during her life or widowhood, four of my negroes, Viz; Ben, Lewis, Shade & Easter. At her death or in the event of her marrying, to be disposed of as above.

Item 4th. I give my wife, one yoke of oxen and wagon and plantation tools, sufficient to work with.

Item 5th. I give my wife, sufficient of my corn, sheep and hogs, for the support of the family, and grain and corn for one year.

Item 6th. I give my wife, two choice work horses and my sorrel filly.

Item. 7th. It is my will and desire that my Executor, hereinafter named, purchase with my money arising from my Estate, sufficient sugar and coffee, for my wife and family one year.

Item 8th. It is my will and desire that my daughters, Elizabeth and Lucy Ann, remain with my wife and be supported out of the Estate, I loan her. If it can be done otherwise, out of their own estate that I shall hereinafter leave them.

Item 9th. It is my will and desire that in the event my daughters should die, without leaving heirs of their own body, then their estate to return and be divided equally among my own children.

Item 10th. It is my will and desire, that the Estate I leave to my daughters, or that they inherit from my estate, at my death, or wife's or marriage, shall go to the heirs of their body.

Item 11th. It is my will and desire, that all my Estate not herein named, shall at my death, be equally divided among all my children.

Item 12th. I appoint David M. Pulley, my son, Executor of this my last will and testament.

In testimony whereof, I have hereunto set my hand and seal this fifteenth day of August, in the year of our Lord, one thousand, eight hundred & thirty seven.

JAMES PULLEY (Seal)

Signed, sealed and delivered
in the presence of
James Abernathy
John H. Price, Jurat
Henry Spear, Jurat

SARAH PYLE

WILL 1841

In the name of God, Amen.

I, Sarah Pyle of Giles, County and State of Tennessee, being of sound and perfect mind & memory, blessed be God, do this the 4th of March, in the year of our Lord, one thousand eight hundred & forty one, make and publish this my last will & testament in the manner following, that is to say,

First, I give and bequeath to my son, Stevin Plesent, one dollar, to him, his heirs and assignee's forever.

Next, I give and bequeath to my son, Demsey Ashford, one dollar, to him and his heirs and assignees forever.

I also give to my son, Willis Ashford, forty dollars, to him, his heirs and assigns forever.

I also give to my son, William Ashford, thirty dollars to him, his heirs and assigns forever.

I also give to my son, James P. Ashford, my bed and bedding, to him, his heirs and assigns forever.

I also give to my daughter, Lucy Pyle, all the balance of my Estate to her and her heirs and assigns forever. And I hereby make and ordain my son in law Henry J. Pyle & John B. Anthony, as Executors of this my last will and testament, in witness I, the said Sarah Pyle, have to this my last will and testament, set my hand and seal the day and year above named. Witnesses, signed, sealed, published and declared by the said Sarah Pyle, the testatrix as her last will and testament in the presence of us who are present at the time of signing and sealing thereof.

her
SARAH X PYLE (Seal)
mark

Test.
William Johnston, Jurat
James Willis, Jurat

SARAH RAINEY

WILL 1842

In the name of God, Amen.

I, Sarah Rainey, wife of Isaac Rainey Sen. Decd. of Bedford County
& State of Tennessee, living in a low state of health, but in sound mind
& memory & being desirous to commit my soul into the hands of Him who
gave it & feeling willing at any time it is his will to go, I resign my
body to the dust from whence it was taken. And as to my temporal property, which it has pleased God to bless me with, I dispose of it in the
following manner.

The portion I may get out of my son, Isaac N. Rainey Estate to be
equally divided between Lemuel Rainey, Patsey Mills, Rachel Lann, Mahala
Lillard & Matilda Dobson, but I desire & direct that Amanda Dodson, shall
have a third part of Matilda's part, also the money Rachel Lane's are to
be divided in the same manner & my bed and furniture. My daughters above
may choose as they please. In testimony whereof, I have hereunto set my
hand and seal this 4th. day of October, 1842.
Signed in the presence of Mary J. Rainey.

her
SARAH X RAINEY
mark

Acknowledged on the 13th in the
presence of,
James H. Gordon, Jurat
James M. Rainey, Jurat

I specially give to Sarah A. Clift, one yarn civerlid, after the
above was assigned.

STEPHEN REDING .

WILL 1830

In the name of God, Amen.

I, Stephen Reding, of Giles County and the State of Tennessee, being of sound mind and memory and in the enjoyment of good health, but knowing that life is uncertain and that death cometh like a thief in the night, being about to travel to distant parts from whence I may never return, I do hereby make and ordain, publish and declair, this following to be my last will and testament.

First; I give my soul to God who gave it, and my body to the dust from whence it was taken, to be decently buried in a Christain like manner by my Executor &. and I desire my just debts, including my funeral expences be first paid, by my Executor, out of my Estate.

Second; I give and bequeath to my beloved wife, Emillia, one ninth part of all my personal and real Estate after the payment of my debts as aforesaid.

Also, I give and bequeath to my daughter, Elizabeth Reding, 25 cents, also my son John Reding, I give and bequeath twenty and one half cents. Also to my son Thomas Reding, one dollar and to my daughter, Mary Gardner I give twenty five cents, also to my daughter Emillia Reding, twenty five cents. I also give to my daughter Susan Reding, twenty dollars.

I also give and bequeath to my two sons, Stephen K. Reding and Henry R. Reding and their heirs, forever all the residue of my estate, both real and personal, not being before disposed to be equally divided between them each to share alike, and if either of my two sons, that is Stephen H. Reding or Henry R. Reding should decease before they arive to the age of twenty one years, I will for the living one to have both shares.

I hereby appoint my esteemed friend and acquaintance, Henry Miller, to execute this my last will and testament. I also hereby appoint him, the said Henry Miller, gardean of the persons Estate of my said sons, Stephen H. and Henry R. Reding, untill they come of full age.

In testimony now, which the said Stephen Reding, do hereby set my hand and seal this twenty ninth day of November 1830.
Interlined before signed.

                                    STEPHEN REDING (Seal)

Signed, sealed, published and declaired
in the presence of each of us, this the
29th day of November 1830.
Test.
Jacob Luther, Jurat
John Beaver, Jurat
Thos. R. Skillern, Jurat

SAMUEL C. REED

WILL 1844

In the name of God, Amen.

I, Samuel C. Reed of Giles County and State of Tennessee, being weak in body but of sound mind and memory, blessed be Almighty God, for same considering the uncertainity of this mortal life, do make this my last will & testament, in manner and form following, that is to say,

First, I give and bequeath unto my beloved wife, all my property, during her widowhood untill my children become of lawful age, after that event, I wish it equally divided among them. The negroes named as follows, handy. It is my will and desire that my wife, if she sees proper to keep house to herself, that she keep such household and kitchen furniture & provisions, full necessary for that purpose. Further it is my will and desire that my present crop and my fattening hogs be sold to make payment of a tract of land I purchased of Mr. Isaac Haney, the balance of my property, including a negro woman. It is my will & desire that they be sold on twelve months credit for the purpose of paying all my debts that may stand against my Estate. Further, it is my will & desire that my father, Thomas Reed, act as Executor to this my last will and testament, and further that he act as Guardian to my children. In witness whereof I have hereunto set my hand and seal this the 11th. day of September 1844.

SAM'L C. REED (Seal)

Test.
David J. Moore, Jurat
Jackson, Coldwell, Jurat
Guston T. Campbell, Jurat

CHRISTOPHER ROBERSON

WILL 1850

In the name of God, Amen.

I, Christopher, do make my last will and testament, towit, but I recommend my soul to God who gave it, my body to be buried in a Christain manner, not doubting but it will be united again at God's appointed time.

First; I bequeath to my brother, Caleb H. Roberson, my negro woman named, Sarah and her children, towit, a boy named Allen, one named Samuel and one named Mieager & one girl, Mourning and one named Roberta, and one saddle and shot gun.

Second; I bequeath to my sister Permelia Hopson, one negro woman named Nellah, to her and her heirs, forever.

I also give to my brother, Caleb H. Roberson, my bed and furniture, to him and his heirs forever. I also leave my negro man named Peter to be sold and equally divided between Permelia Hopson, Moses Roberson, & Rawley W. Roberson. I also leave the ballance of my property to be sold and to pay my just debts, and if any over, to be divided between my two brothers and sisters above named. Which this is my last will and testament and appoint my brother, Caleb H. Roberson and John Hobson, of Virginia to be my Executors to my will.

his

CHRISTOPHER L. X ROBERSON (Seal)

mark

Signed in presence of
John Carmichael, Jurat
Simon Pearson, Jurat

DENNY ROPER

WILL 1845

I, Denny Roper, widow, being in a feble state of health do make and publish this as my last will and testament, hereby first, I direct that my funeral Expences and all my debts be paid as soon after my death as possible out of any money that I may die possessed of, or may first come into the hands of my son, James C. Roper, of my assets.

Secondly, I give and bequeath to my said son, James C. Roper, my negro woman, Nancy, all of my horses, cattle, sheep, hogs, oxen & ox cart, and twelve acres of land, Entered by General Location in Giles County, adjoining my dower on the south and Silas L. Veach's north boundary.

In witness whereof, I do to this my will, set my hand and seal this 13th day of November, 1845.

DENNY ROPER (Seal)

Signed, sealed and published
in our presence and we have
subscribed our names hereto
in the presence of the testators
this 15th day of November 1845

R.G. Abernathy, Jurat
John Y. Abernathy, Jurat

JOSEPH ROWE

WILL 1845

State of Tennessee)
Giles County   )   September 25th 1845
    Know all men by these present that I, Joseph Rowe, of the state and
County above mentioned, do this day make this, my last will and testament, viz; To Eleazar, my son and Mary my wife, during her natural life,
the premises on which I now live, extending west to a line to commence
at Alfred Rowe's north west corner, running north to the Bear Camp branch,
thence west to the little rock spring, thence north to the north boundary
of the tract. To my son Miles, I give all the land contained in the original tract west of Eliezar's west line as above mentioned. To my son,
Alfred, I give the land lying south of the line running east from Alfred
Rowe's north west corner, so as to include the land I purchased from Elam
Stevenson. To my son Henry, I give the entire tract of land I purchased
from Devories Hightower, lying in Lincoln County, Tenn. To my son, Joseph
I give all the land I purchased from Morgan Holbert and Philemon Higgins
lying in Lincoln County, Tennessee. Furthermore I leave Benjamin Smith
my son in law five dollars. I leave Wm. Stevenson my son in law five
dollars. I leave Henry Rowe, my son, five dollars. I leave Alfred Rowe,
my son, five dollars. I leave Benjamin Bass, my son in law, five dollars.
I leave my son, Joseph, the sorrel horse that he claims. I leave my son
Miles, the bay horse that he claims. I leave Eliezar, my son, thirty one
dollars to buy a horse for him. I leave to Polly, my wife the sorrel
mare that she claims. I leave my son, Miles one hundred and fifty dollars
extra, for building on his land. I leave my son, Eliezar, my shot gun.
I leave the remainder of all my stock to my wife, Polly and my sons,
Joseph, Miles and Eliezar, to be divided equally among them.
                                        his
                          JOSEPH X ROWE (Seal)
                                        mark

Attest.
A.M. Pickens,
Larkin Gardin, Jurat
Jacob Hart
Elisha Bennett, Jurat

EDMUND SHELTON

WILL 1846

State of Tennessee)
Giles County   )

I, Edmund Shelton, being of sound mind and disposing memory, do make ordain and publish, this my last will and testament, in manner and form following;

First; be it known that I have given to each one of my living children this present year a portion of property amounting to five hundred and seventy five dollars. And it is my will that my daughter, Sarah Whitmore's children, George, Mary and Susan, at my death draw from my Estate, the sum of five hundred and seventy five dollars, together with the lawful interest on the same from the first day of January next. After that it is my will that the balance of my property be equally divided, among all my children, my three above named grand children coming in for one share.

Lastly; I hereby appoint my sons, Thomas P. Shelton, James H. Shelton and Robert P. Shelton, Executor of this, my last will and testament, revoking all former wills by me made. In witness whereof I have hereunto set my hand and affixed my seal, this the 26th day of June, 1846.

EDMUND SHELTON (Seal)

Witnesses;
Joseph F. Brown, Jurat
Elizabeth M. Wilson
William J. Tarpley, Jurat
Early Benson

BUCKNER SMITH

WILL 1818

State of Tennessee and County of Giles.

I, Buckner Smith, being sick in body but of sound mind and memory, do make this my last will and testament, In the manner and form following;

First; My soul to Almighty God who gave it & my body to the dust.

Second; My property to be divided as follows, say the land where I now live, my beloved wife, Dianna to live on it as long as she lives & horses, cows, hogs & stock of all kinds to remain with her for her support & the children that are now with us unmarried & at her death the said land & stock on hand to be sold and equally divided between all my children, but my negroes to be divided as follows; Say my son, Leonard to have as his right & property a negro by the name of Adam & also a colt by the name of Stars, also a saddle that now is in his possession. I further desire that my son, Robert should have a negro girl of mine by his paying to my Estate three hundred dollars, then the negro girl, Ester to be his right and property & to have the bed that is now claimed by him in my house, with its furniture, now in there possession, to have as their own property, also the negro woman Eady & her increase, hereafter at the death of my beloved wife to be equally devided. Also I wish my son James to have a bed, I wish my son Robert James to live on the land and work together & support my beloved wife and daughters, that is with them & have what they make over to themselves, as their own. As witness I appoint my son, Robert Executor of my Estate, witness my hand & the Lord have mercy on me. Feb. 3rd. 1818.

                                        his
                            BUCKNER X SMITH (Seal)
                                        mark

Tests.
James Flaut
John Young
Wm. Harwell $1 paid

JOHN SMITH

WILL 1818

In the name of God, Amen.

I, John Smith of the State of Tennessee and County of Giles, being weak in body, yet of a sound mind and perfect understanding & memory do constitute and ordain this my last will and Testament.

My wish and desire is in the place that all my just and lawful debts of which there is but few, and none of magnitude, should be paid as soon as convenient. Also I do give and bequeath unto my beloved wife, Cathrine forever, all my property in the following manner. I wish all my stock to be sold, only one cow and calf to be reserved for her use, and the money to be put to her suport. Also I do give and bequeath unto my beloved wife, Cathrine, all my lands and tenements lying in the County and State aforesaid with all the appurtenences belonging thereunto to dispose of as she may think proper.

Lastly; I do make and constitute Duncan Brown and Elesear Purvance, Executors of this my last will and testament. In witness whereof, I do here set my hand and seal dated this the 30th of April 1818.

JOHN SMITH (Seal)

Tests.
John Brown, Jurat
Daniel M. Collins, Jurat

JOHN W. SMITH

WILL 1837

I, John W. Smith of the County of Giles and State of Tennessee, being sound in mind but of diseased body, Do make and constitute this my last will and testimony. In the name of God, Amen, I do make and constitute dear wife, Mary Eliza Smith, and my friend, Benjamin Carter, my Executrix and Executor, with full power to sell any of my property, either real or personal and to purchase with the proceeds any other property which they may think advantageous to my family. It is my request that my slaves should not be hired out but kept together on my farm. I give and bequeath to my dear wife, Mary Eliza Smith, during her lifetime, all my property both real and personal, but with the request that as my two dear sons becomes of age, she divide with them the property, as she may find it convenient, reserving to herself at least one third of it, or more, should she think she needed that much, Except at some time my dear wife, Mary Elizabeth Smith should intermarry with another person, in which case, but (God forbid it) then I will and bequeath all my property both real and personal to be equally divided between her and my two sons, James F. Smith and John Congan Smith, shear and shear alike.

In testimony whereof, I have subscribed my name and afixed my seal this the 11th of February, 1837.

JOHN W. SMITH

Witness
J.J.P. Lindsay
James Johnston

MARGARET STOCKDON

WILL 1818

September 12th 1818.
In the name of God, Amen.

    I first recommend my soul to God and my body to be buried at the disposal of my friend, and being weak in body but sound in mind and make this my last will and say that Benjamin Stockdon, my son shall have five shillings if ever aplied for. It is further my wish and will that the children of Elizabeth Stockdon, William Stockdon, Josiah Stockdon, Margaret Stockdon, Lucinda Stockdon & Smith Stockdon, my personal property to be eculy divided amongst the above named children, excepe a small ———————— to Margaret Stockdon, thease being my grandchildy.

                                    her
                        MARGARET X STOCKDON
                              mark

Test
Davis Brown
Zebulon Rainey
Samuel Newton

THOMAS C. STONE

WILL 1844

In the name of God, Amen.

I, Thomas C. Stone, of the County of Giles and State of Tennessee, being sick and infirm of body, but of sound mind and memory, do make this my last will and testament in manner and form following; Viz;

Item 1st. I lend unto my beloved wife, Jane, during her natural life, five negro slaves viz, Wyche, Joe, Fletcher, Nancy, Sr, and Nancy Jr. and also the land and premises on which I now reside, one gray mare, one sorrel mare, called Kit, one yoke of oxen, one wagon, four cow & calves three thousand pounds of pork, twenty five choice stock hogs, twenty head of sheep, household and kitchen furniture, one bed and furniture excepted.

Item 2nd. I give unto my daughter, Mary H. Stone, one negro girl (slave) name Minerva and her increase, one bay mare (Called Lucy) One bed and furniture, one cow and calf and one side saddle, the same being about the value already given to each of my other heirs, Jane Nave excepted.

Item 3rd. I lend unto my daughter, Jane Nave, one negro girl, slave named Alcy, and her increase, during her natural life, and at her death shall belong to her legal heirs of her body, forever. It is also my will and desire that the portion of my estate, drawn by my daughter, Jane Nave, as a legatee (not herein mentioned, shall be in money which shall be placed in the hands of Thomas J. Stone, for the purpose of purchasing a negro, which negro shall be loaned to her during her natural life and at her death shall belong to the legal heirs of her body, forever.

Item 4th. It is my will and desire that my daughter, Elizabeth D. Chamblin, shall have the use and services of my negro woman, Eady, during her natural life of my wife and at her decease said negro shall be returned to my Estate. It is also my will and desire that the portion drawn by said Elizabeth, shallbe in money, which money shall be placed in the hands of John C. Stone, for the purpose of purchasing a negro girl, which negro and her increase shall be loaned to her during her natural life, and at her death shall be given to the legal heirs of her body forever.

Item 5th. It is my will and desire that my land, known as the Peden tract, and the remaining portion of the Edwards tract and all other property not herein mentioned, belonging to me (after paying my debts, be equally divided between my children and Charles E. Verelle, my stepson.

I do hereby nominate my wife, Jane, and my son Thomas J. Stone, the sole Executors of this my last will and testament, hereby revoking all other wills by me made.

In witness whereof, I have hereunto set my hand and seal this the eleventh day of March in the year of our Lord, one thousand eight hundred and forty four.

THOS. C. STONE

Signed, sealed & delivered
in the presence of
Benjamin M. Coggins, Jurat
B.R. Field, Jurat

ANDREW E.Y. TACKER

WILL 1857

I, Andrew E.Y. Tacker, of the County of Giles, and State of Tennessee
do make and ordain the following, as my last will and testament, hereby
revoking and declaring void, all other wills by me at any time heretofore
made.

First. I will and direct that my funeral expenses and all my just
debts be paid out of my monies, I may die possessed of or that may first
come into the hands of my Executor, after my death.

Secondly; It is my will that my children remain together and continue
to occupy, untill raised, my residence. And my Executor is hereby directed in order to carry out this provision of my will, to retain unsold the
following specified articles of property, towit, my tract of land, known
as the home tract, containing about one hundred and ten acres, one years
provision, my gray mare about twenty years of age, two bay mares, one six
years of age, the other three years old and one black filly, about one
year old, two cows and calves and such stock, hogs and sheep as in his
opinion may be necessary, one wagon and harness, six feather beds, and
furniture and such other household and kitchen furniture as may be needed
for the support and comfort of my said children. all necessary plantation
utensils, one loom and weaving gear, two spinning wheels, cards, &.

Thirdly; Having confidence in my son, William R. Tacker, the eldest
of my six children. I desire that my Executor place him in possession
of the land and other property above specified for the purpose of raising
and schooling my other children, and the joint support of them and him
untill the youngest child shall come of age or marry. And it is further
my will that my said son shall have in his own right all that he may be
able to make from said farm and other property after a support and
schooling of my other children, this arrangement to continue while in
the opinion of my Executor, the said William R. shall so manage the property and provide for the support of my other children as herein contem-
plated and no longer.

Fourthly; It is my will that my children, towit; William R. Elizabeth
J., Violet I., Rebecca U., Mary S. and Hester Ann, shall each, as they
shall arrive at the age of twenty one years or marry, draw from, and my
Executor is hereby directed to pay over to them an equal distributive
share of such means, belonging to my estate as shall be in his hands,
not interfering however with such portion of my Estate as is hereby set
apart for their General support and raising.

Fifthly; It is my will that the residue of my property, that is
such as is not herein otherwise directed to be used, be sold upon the
following terms, towit, The perishable property upon a credit of twelve
months without interest, my negro man, Allen to be sold on one and two
years credit, with interest from date and my tract of land, known as the
Locke tract upon a credit of one, two, and three years time with interest
upon the whole from date and my Executor is hereby empowered to make sale
of said property and to make and execute a bill of sale to said negro and
the deed for said land to the purchaser, which title so made shall be good
without reference to expensive legal proceedings and the assets arising
from said sale to remain in the hands of my Executor as means for the payment of my debts or for distribution amongst my children as above

directed.

Sixthly: It is my will that when my youngest child shall arrive at the age of twenty one years or shall marry, my Executor is directed to sell the residue and remainder of my estate of whatever kind, the perishable property and on twelve months time, and the land on one and two years with interest from date and make equal distribution of the same amongst my children share and share alike, he selling and executing a title and deed to the land without refrences to decrees of court or legal proceedings as before directed.

Seventhly: I will and bequeath to my son, William R. my watch as a special legacy and hereby wave all claims to such pork and stock hogs as are distinguished as his on my place.

Lastly: I hereby nominate and appoint my friend and Brother, William R. Tacker, my Executor to this my will.

(Interlined be ore assigned)

In witness whereof I hereunto set my hand and seal this 25th day of Oct. 1859.

                                        A.E.Y. TACKER (Seal)

Signed, sealed, published and declared
to be his last will and testament in
the presence of us on 25th Oct. 1859.
Thos. R.E. Boatright
William Evans

JOSHUA TACKER

WILL, 1848

The last will and testament of Joshua Tacker.

 I, Joshua Tacker, considering the uncertainity of this mortal life, and being of sound mind and memory, do make and publish this my last will and testament in manner and form following, That is to say first, I give and bequeath to my beloved wife, Susan, all my land, Estate except forty acres, I will and give to my son, Jacob, to be laid of as follows; beginning on John Harwell's line, in the creek running with it, north to my cotton patch fence, then running with said fence as a line to Reed's line. I will to my wife all my stock of hogs, cattle and horses, except one yoak of oxen I will and give to my son John. I further will and give to my wife all my household and kitchen furniture and then at her death all to be sold and equally divided between my children. I hereby appoint my wife sole Executrix of this my last will and testament. In witness whereof I have set my hand and seal this 18th day of May, 1848.

her
JOSHUA X TACKER (Seal)
mark

Levi Reed, Jurat
John Harwell, Jurat

GEORGE TAYLOR.

WILL 1842

I, George Taylor, do make and publish this as my last will and Testament hereby revoking and making void all other wills by me at any time made.

First; I direct that my funeral expences and all my debts be paid as soon as possible out of any money that I may die possessed of or may first come into the hands of my Executors.

Secondly; I give and bequeath to my wife, Elizabeth Taylor, all my property after paying my debts as above stated, viz; My house and land and negro woman, America, her son a negro boy named Mayer, and my negro man Ralph, and a girl named Phillis, also my money notes, and accounts and live stock of all kinds, also the household and kitchen furniture, to have and to hold so long as she may live to the use of her support. And at my wife, Elizabeth Taylors death, I desire that my Estate be equally divided between my two daughters viz; Mary Worsham, wife of William Worsham, and Martha Worsham, wife of John Worsham, their heirs and assigns forever, Morever I give and bequeath to my daughter, Martha Worsham, the dwelling house of John Worsham decd. now standing on my premises, to dwell in so long as she may remain single to have and to hold as hir own house.

Lastly, I do hereby nominate and appoint my Executors in witness whereof I do to this my will, set my hand and seal this 5th day of April 1842.

                                        his
                              GEORGE X TAYLOR
                                        mark

Signed, sealed and published
in our presence and we have
subscribed our names hereto
in the presence of the testators this 5th day of April 1842.
Tests,
William Lackey, Jurat (Seal)
Granville, R. Lester, Jurat (Seal)
John Craven, Jurat

DAVID THOMSON

WILL 1851

In the name of God, Amen.

I, David Thomson, of this County of Giles and State of Tennessee, being low in body, but of sound mind and memory, do make and ordain this to be my last will and Testament, revoking all others heretofore by me made, and in manner and form following, towit; I give and bequeath unto my son Thomas F. Thomson, a negro woman named, Clementine, and her son Jesse, also a negro woman named Kate, and her son, Robert, and their future increase to him and his heirs and assigns forever.

2nd. I give and bequeath unto my son in law, William E. Johnson, a negro man named Dilley, and his wife, Nancy, and their son, Bolen, to him, his heirs & assigns, forever.

3rd. I give and bequeath unto my son, Robert B. Thomson, a negro boy named, William, to him, his heirs and assigns forever.

4th. I give and bequeath unto my daughter, Judith B. Thomson, a negro girl named Rachel, with her future increase to her, her heirs and assigns forever.

5th. I give and bequeath unto John W. Thomson, my son, a negro boy named, Sandy, to him, his heirs and assigns forever.

6th. I give and bequeath unto my son, James L. Thomson, a negro boy, named Henry, to him, his heirs and assigns forever.

7th. I give and bequeath unto my son, William H. Thomson, a negro boy, named Dick, to him, his heirs and assigns forever.

8th. It is my will and desire that the tract of land whereon I now live, be sold by my Executors in the way and manner they may think best, and I do by these present give full power and authority to my Executors hereafter named, or any one of them to make a deed to the same so soon as a sale thereof is effected.

9th. It is my will and desire that the plantation be under the direction and care of my son, Thomas E. Thomson, during this year and the rpoceeds of the farm applied to the payment of my debts.

10th. All my stock of every description, plantation utensils, household and kitchen furniture (except a bed and furniture to each of my following named children, Robert, Judith, John, James, & William, be sold on a credit of twelve months, and my youngest son, William may receive twenty five in the place of a bed & furniture which I suppose will be about equal.

11th. It is my will further that out of the proceeds of the sale of my Estate that twelve hundred dollars be appropriated as follows; namely, three hundred dollars to David T. Freeman, three hundred dollars to Winnifred S. Ware and the balance of the money my Estate sells for to be equally divided among all my children & sons in law named above. I leave my son, Thomas E. Thomson, son, Robert Thomson & son in law, William E. Johnson, Executors, to this my last will & testament. And it is my will that they act on my estate without being reqruirred to give security or make any return to court whatever. Further the proving and recording this will in testimony whereof, I have hereunto set my hand & affixed my seal, this 30th. day of April, 1851.

DAVID THOMSON (Seal)

Thos. E. Abernathy, J.
Thos. E. Daly, J.

WILLIAM TRIGG

WILL, 1839

In the name of God, Amen.

I, William Trigg of Giles County Tennessee, being in ill health but
of perfect mind and sound memory (thanks be given to God for these mercies)
calling to mind the mortality of my body, and knowing that it is appointed
for all men once to die, do make and ordain this my last will and testament that is to say, principally and first of all I give and recommend
my soul into the hands of Almighty God that gave it, and my body I recommend to the earth to be buried in a decent Christain manner at the discretion of my Executors, not doubting but at the general Resurrection I
shall receive the same again by the mighty power of God.

First; I give and bequeath to my dearly beloved wife, Nancy Trigg,
the Plantation, whereon I now live to her, during her life, and in addition to this, I bequeath to her all my stock consisting of horses, cows,
hogs and sheep. I also bequeath to her all the farming utensils, belonging
to the farm, and all household and kitchen furniture, during her life.

I bequeath to my son, Ira the sum of five dollars, also to my son
David, the sum of one hundred dollars. The above sums of money to be paid
at the death of my wife. I also bequeath to my son, John, a horse and
bed , when he arrives at the age of twenty one years, or at the discretion
of my wife, Nancy Trigg. I also want my son John to have one years schooling before he becomes twenty one years of age. I will further add that
if my son, John will remain on the farm with his mother, he shall be entitled to all he can make by his own industry, and the remainder of my
estate at the death of my wife to be equally divided amongst my seven
children to viz; David, Mary Ann, Susanah H, Drucila, Hiram, William L.
and John. And lastly I hereby nominate my wife, Nancy and my son, John
my executrix & Executor , this is my last will and testament. In witness
whereof I have hereunto set my hand and seal this 30th day of October in
the year of our Lord one thousand eight hundred and thirty nine.

WM. TRIGG (Seal)

Tests
James Derr, Jurat
Paul Chiles, Jurat
Wm. D. Orr, Jurat

GEORGE B. TUCKER

WILL 1859

I, George B. Tucker, of sound mind and disposing memory, do make this my last will and testament, hereby revoking all other wills by me made at any time previous to this.

First; I direct my body decently but not expensively intered and the expense of which paid by my Eoecutor, hereafter mentioned with the first money that comes in his hands.

Secondly; My debts all paid with the means and effects in my possession owing to me, and if that should lack of paying them off, my Executor pay the balance with the surplus of my estate. And it is my will and desire, my widow, Margaret Tucker occupy my freehold now owned by me of about seventy acres, during her natural life and so much of the household and kitchen furniture, as well as stock & provisions as she may need and desire for her comfort and suport during her natural life.

I bequeath to my daughter, Rebecca Tucker, out of the surplus not absolutely needed by my said widow, if there be a surplus sufficient to make, if not to come out of my real estate the sum of two hundred and fifty dollars as a renumeration of her long and continued care and probation of myself and her mother as one of the family. My said widow is to retain, during her natural life all my land as above specified as a home, for and during her natural life, and at her death, It is my desire that my Executors sell to the highest bidder the above named premises and the household and kitchen furniture & other effects by me left to my said widow and an equal distribution made between all my children, exceptI wish them who have not as yet received a horse, who are my daughters, Elenor Kyle, widow of Wm. P. Kyle, and Lenny H. Campbell, wife of Gustus T. Campbell, and Lunary Bee, wife of Wm. Bee, and Rebecca Tucker, each receive in lein of the horse each of the others have received Thirty dollars. And it is my desire and will that my sons, M.B. Tucker, and John R.C. who have not as yet received no bed, to receive each in lein of the bed, ten dollars, after all the above Legacies are paid, as above specified, then the balance and residue of my entire Estate be equally divided among my children.

Lastly, I nominate and appoint my sons, Daniel A. and M.R. Tucker, my Executors, to Execute this my last will and testament, this October 25th 1859.

Geo. B. Tucker (Seal)

Joseph L. Edmundson
Richard R. Meadows

WILL T. TUCKER.

WILL 1857

We, Francis Fergerson and Daniel F. Collins, do state that the non-occupative will of Will T. Tucker was made by him on the 7th. day of May 1857 in our presence, to which we were specially requested to bear witness by the testor himself in the presence of each other, that it was made in his last sickness in his own dwelling and that the same is as follows, to-wit, that his affets should be disposed of in the following manner; After his decease, first, that all his just debts should be paid; Second, that his mother, Nancy Tucker should have all the balance of his money, and also a set cheny he gave to his brother, Henry J. Tucker, one mare, saddle and bridle, his hogs he gave to be equally divided between his mother, Nancy Tucker and Reuben G. Tucker and Henry J. Tucker, his growing crop he gave to be equally divided between his father, Tommas N. Tucker, his mother, Nancy Tucker, and Richard G. Tucker and Henry J. Tucker, the legaces he gave to his mother Nancy Tucker and Henry J. Tucker, he gave into the hands of his brother, Richard G. Tucker, for their benefit. Made out and signed by us this 15th of May 1857.

FRANCIS FERGERSON
DANIEL F. COLLINS

JONAS VICK

WILL 1840

In the name of God, Amen.

I, Jonas Vick, of the County of Giles and state of Tennessee, considering the uncertainity of this mortal life, & being of sound and perfect mind and memory, Blessed be God for the same, do make and publish this, my last will and testament in manner and form following.

First: I give and bequeath unto my son, Alen T. Vick, all my land with the exception of fifty acres off of the north end of my land, which I give and bequeath to my son, Wesley J. Vick, unless he should prefer my bay horse to the fifty acres of land, then the land shall be A.T. Vick's, furthermore I give and bequeath unto my son, Alen T. Vick, all my other property with the exception of those five cows chosen by my five daughters The geese also belong to my daughters & all the household property not mentioned in the will, to the said A.T. Vick in connection with what has been divided out to his sisters, is bound by this will, to school his three younger sisters and also his sister, Jane, if she chooses to go to school also to keep them together as a family and provide for them, such as he has for himself, untill they leave the family by marriage or mutual consent. He shall furnish them each with a bead a ewe and lambs, and a sow & pigs. He is also bound to keep the land untill the youngest child is of age in order that their mantainance be secured to them. I hereby nominate and appoint my son Alen T. Vick, Executor of this my last will & testament.

In witness whereof I have hereunto set my hand & seal this the 9th day of April 1840.

                                        her
                                JONAS   VICK
                                        mark

Signed, sealed, published & delivered
by the above named Jonas Vick, to be
his last will & Testament
Testators,
David G. Crockett
Washington Armour, Jr.

JOHN WAGSTAFF

WILL 1838

State of Tennessee)
Giles County)
September the 15th 1838)

I, John Wagstaff, Bequeath of my Estate to so much as will pay all my debts. I also bequeath to my wife, Mary Wagstaff, all the property that I have to help rase the children and to school them, towit, Elizabeth, Selina, Bazzle, William, Rebecca, Maryan, John Randol, Robert Darnel, Leathy Jane & James, so long as shee remains my widdow.

I bequeath to my son, John Randol, to have one horse, bridle, & saddle to be worth one hundred dollars, when he becomes of age, provided he stay with my wife till he is twenty one years of age. I also give and bequeath to my son, Robert Daniel one horse, bridle & saddle, worth one hundred dollars when he becomes of age of twenty one, if he stays with wife till he is twenty one years of age, also. I also bequeath to my son, James, one horse, bridle & saddle, when he becomes of the age of twenty one years, & stays with my wife till he is twenty one years old. I also bequeath to Rebeker, my daughter & give to her one new saddle, one cow and calf & one bed & furniture and fifty dollars in cash. I also bequeath to my daughter, Maryan, one new saddle, one bed and furniture, one cow and calf and fifty dollars in cash. I also bequeath to my daughter, Leathy Jane, one new saddlem one bed & furniture, one cow and calf, & fifty dollars in cash. I also want my wife, Mary Wagstaff & Bazzley Wagstaff to Administer on my Estate & also to be appointed gargens of all my children that is under twenty one years old. I also will & Bequeath all of my Estate that is coming to me from my fathers Estate to all my children, to be equally divided between them. I also bequeath to my wife & my son, Bazzley, the liberty of moving the property anywhere they think proper and also to sell two negroes to buy land with to keep my children together on. I also want the Estate coming to me from my father's estate to fall into the hands & remain in the hands of my wife & my son, Bazzley, as my other property does. I, John Wagstaff, do will and bequeath that of my last will & Testament that at the death of my wife, I want all my Estate devided between my ten children or if my wife should marry, I want my Estate to be equally divided between my ten children. In witness to this I now subscrib my last will and testament.

                                        JOHN WAGSTAFF (Seal)

Tests
L.J. McKissack, Jurat
John P. Taylor, Jurat
Henry McCormack

BENJAMIN WHEELER

WILL 1842

In the name of God, Amen.

I, Benjamin Wheeler, of the County of Giles and State of Tennessee, being of sound mind and memory, but knowing that is appointed for all men once to die, and being desirous to prepare for so important and solemn event, Do make my last will and testament, hereby revoking and disannulling any and all former wills by me made.

In the first place, it is my will and desire that my daughter, Sarah receive a bed, bed furniture, to make her equal with my married daughter, and in addition to this, I will that my daughter, Sarah, have the following property as she has gained it by her industry, viz; two good beds and furniture, two pair of bedsteads, one bureau, one chest, one candlestand, one bay mare, saddle and bridle, in the next place, I desire and will that after my death, my wife, Nancy Wheeler, shall have and enjoy the whole of my property, real and personal, during her natural life and at her death, I direct that the whole shall be sold and equally divided among all my legal heirs with this proviso, nevertheless that my said wife, Nancy shall have the liberty of disposing of the household furniture in such manner as to her may seem best.

In testimony whereof I have hereunto set my hand and seal this the 31st day of August 1842.

BENJAMIN WHEELER (Seal)

Attest.
F.W. Hill, Jurat
John R. Hill, Jurat

NANCY WHEELER

WILL 1853

I, Nancy Wheeler, do make and publish this as my last will and Testament.

First, I direct that my funeral expenses and all my debts be paid as soon after my death as possible, out of any money that I may die possessed of or may first come into the hands of my Executor.

2nd. I give and bequeath unto my son, Benjamin F. Wheeler, all the property that I may die possessed of, of every description both real and personal.

In witness whereof I do to this will set my hand and seal this the 29th day of November, one thousand eight hundred and fifty three, (1853)

                                        her
                              NANCY X WHEELER (Seal)
                                        mark

F.W. Hill, X
J.E. Parson, X

TABITHA WILKINS

WILL 1817

December the 2nd. 1817
In the name of God, Amen.

I, Tabitha Wilkins, of the County of Giles, do make and ordain this my last will and testament in manner and form as follows, towit;

Item 1st. I leave Adaline Purnell and Amanda Purnell and Mary Chambers and Elige Cooke, to each of them one dousen silver tablespoons and one dousen teaspoons to be paid for with the money that William Purnell owes for the land.

Item 2nd. I leave T.M. Morthesnfish, one hundred dollars, and one bed and one cow and calf. I leave one hundred dollars to be put in the bank and the interest to be drawn, every year for the airkit preacher in Daniel Martindale's society and if that should breakm I leave it to the preacher in the poorest society in the neighborhood.

Item 3rd. If they should join to build a meetinghouse in the neighborhood. I leave fifty dollars toward it, I leave Annykey, twenty five dollars as she is not free. I leave all the rest of my estate to my son Benjamin Wilkins, and if he never returns I desire, Lidey, and Mingo and Nancy, and Annkey, if she is free , to be maintained out of it as long as they live, and then what is left to Adeline and Mandy Purnell. My desire that John Hawkins & Guston Kearney should be my Executors.

In witness my hand and seal.

TABITHA WILKINS (Seal)

Test.
David Sims, Jurat

MARGARET WILLIAMS

WILL 1854

I, Margaret Williams, wife of John Williams, of the County of Giles and State of Tennessee, being in feeble health but of sound and disposing mind, do make and publish this instrument as my last will and testament, hereby revoking all wills by me, heretofore made.

It is my will and desire and I do hereby direct that all my property real and personal of every discription be sold and converted into money by my Executors, hereinafter appointed and in such way as in his judgement will most advanced and promote the interest of the devisees and Legatees, to whom the same is by this will given.

My said property consists of land, negroes, chattels. I will and bequeath all my above mentioned Estate to my two grandchildren, Volney and Virginia, Cyrus, children of my son, Charles B. Cyrus, to be equally divided between them, but I will and direct that my son Charles B. Cyrus, have the use and benefit of the annual proffits and income or interest accruing from the proceeds of the sale of my estate as aforesaid and that my Executors, pay over the same to be used by him as he may think proper and to be absolutely his own as long as he lives. And it is my will and I hereby direct that if either of the above named grandchildren shall die without issue that the survivor of them shall have and be entitled to the whole of my said above mentioned and discribed Estate, to him or her and his or her children forever, and further it is my will and desire and I hereby direct that if both my said above named grandchildren shall die without leaving a child or children, that in that event the whole Estate above devised and bequeathed to them shall become the property of the children of my brother, William and Lewis Conner, and I hereby in that contingency, give and bequeath the same to them. My health having been very bad and feeble for many years, should it be the will of providence that I should for a length of time continue to linger in feeble health, it is my will and I hereby empower and direct my Executors to pay to my husband, John Williams, out of my Estate, such sum of money as in his opinion will amply compensate him for his trouble and kind care and attention to me, which I doubt not he will continue to extend me as long as I live. I will and direct that the money arising from the sale of my Estate, as aforesaid be kept at lawful interest by my Executors, and the interest so accruing be paid over by him annually to my son, Charles B. Cyrus, as above directed. I will and direct that if the said Charles B. Cyrus should die during the minority of my said grandchildren, that my Executor pay over to them, the whole of my Estate, when they arrive at lawful age, or the one half to the said Virginia upon her marriage. I hereby appoint my brother, William Conner, my sole Executor, to execute this my last will and testament. In testimony whereof, I have hereto set my hand and seal this 14th day of December, A.D. 1853.

her

MARGARET X WILLIAMS (Seal)

mark

Test.
Wm. A. Jones, Jurat
James L. Gooch, Jurat

THOMAS WILLIAMS

WILL 1849

I, Thomas Williams, of the County of Giles and State of Tennessee, being weak in body but of sound and disposing mind, do make and ordain this my last will and testament in manner and form following;

Item 1st. I give and bequeath to my beloved wife, Susan Williams, during her life, the south part of the tract of land on which I now live, containing one hundred and seventy six acres agreable to a late survey, made by Nelson Patteson and at the death of my said wife, my will is that said land be sold on a credit of four equal anual payments and the proceeds arrising from said sale, I wish equally divided amongst my children, Steven, Williams, Samuel Williams, Franklin Williams, Caroline Adams, Sarah Williams, & Katharine Williams.

Item 2nd. I give and bequeath to my said wife, during her lifetime two negro women, named Matilda & Charlotte and one girl name, Mary, one man nom Sam, all my household and kitchen furniture to dispose of as she may think proper, two choice plows, 1 choice harrow, three choice hoes, three choice axes, Also my ox wagon and two yokes of oxen, twenty head of my best hogs, and provisions enough to last her one year.

Item 3rd. My will and desire is that the tract of land, Harris Rainey now lives on, if not complice with agreable to an obligation that William D. Abernathy, has in possession if said Rainey does not comply with the said obligation. It is my desire that said tract of land be sold agreable to the obligation with bond approved security and the proceeds equally divided amongst my said children, Steven Williams, Franklin Williams, Samuel Williams, Caroline Adams, Sarah Williams, & Katherine Williams.

Item 4th. I give and bequeath to my son, John Williams, all of my tract of land lying on the north side of said survey made by said Patteson Also I give and bequeath to him, one negro man name, Bradly to him and his heirs forever.

Item 5th. It is my will and desire that my daughters, Sarah and Katharine Williams, have one hundred dollars each out of the first money on hand, extra of their equal share. I hereby appoint my brother in law William S. Samuel and William T. Adams, my son in law, Executors to this my last will and testament. In testimony whereof, I have hereunto set my name and affixed my seal this 19th. day of January A.D. 1848.

THOMAS WILLIAMS (Seal)

Test.
Wm. D. Marks, Jurat
George Everly, Jurat

BRITTON YARBROUGH

WILL 1815

In the name of God, Amen.

I, Britton Yarbrough of the County of Giles, being of sound mind and memory, (blessed be God) do this nineteenth day of October, In the year of our Lord, one thousand, eight hundred and fifteen make and publish this my last will and Testament, in manner and form following, that is to say

First; I allow my gray mare and six head of cattle and five head of sheep to be sold to raise money to pay my debts, and if that should not be sufficient I allow my Executor to sell that part of the property that in his opinion can be best spared to make up the deficiency.

Secondly; I give and bequeath to my beloved wife, Polly, all the rest of my property that remains after my just debts are paid, to her own use and that of my children and to act with it as her and my Executor may think best for the advantage of my wife and children. And I hereby make and ordain my worthy brother Ambrose Yearbrough Executor of this my last will and Testament. In witness whereof the said Britton Yarbrough, have to this my last will and testament set my hand and seal the day and date above written.

BRITON YARBROUGH (Seal)

Signed, sealed published and declaired
by the said Briton Yarbrough, the
testator as his last will and testament
in the presence of us who were present
at the time of signing & sealing
thereof.
J? Henderson
John Maxwell
Jesse Vanhooser.   1815

DAVID YARBROUGH

WILL 1841

In the name of God, Amen.

I, David Yarbrough, of the Town of Marion, County of Perry, and State of Alabama, being mindful of my mortality and being of sound mind and disposing memory, do this the eighteenth day of September in the year of our Lord, one thousand eight hundred and forty one, make and publish this my last will and testament.

First: I desire to be decently buried at the discretion of my Executors hereinafter named.

Item 1st; It is my will and desire that all my property, real and personal in the State of Alabama, except my negroes and my house and lot in the Town of Marion, Perry County in which I now reside, be sold by my Executors upon the usual credit and that the proceeds be applied to the payments of my just debts.

Item 2nd. I will and bequeath to my grand daughter Mary Hardy Alston, a negro girl names Peggy, daughter of Emeline, and five hundred dollars in cash to be paid by my Executors out of the monies arising from the sale of the property above directed to be sold.

Item 3rd. I will and bequeath to my grand daughter, Annie S.J. Alston a negro girl named Mary, daughter of Princess, and five hundred dollars in cash to be raised and paid out of the property above directed to be sold.

Item Fourth; I give and bequeath to my Grand son Henry Y. Foster, two negro boys, Charles and Calvin.

Item fifth; I give and bequeath to my Grand son David Y. Houze, two boys, Amos and Johnson.

Item sixth; I give and bequeath to my beloved wife, Hellen W. Yarbrough my house and lot in the Town of Marion in which I now reside, and one third of the residue of my negroes not bequeathed to my grandchildren, according to valuation, to be valued by impartial persons & to be selected by my wife in families as far as practicable.

Item seventh; I will and bequeath to my friends, Leonard A. Weissinger Geo. T. Johnson, & Wm. F. Studwick, in trust for the use, benefit and support of my beloved daughter, Frances D. Foster, one third part of my negroes (according to value) not bequeathed to my grandchildren to be held in trust by the said Trustees for the sole use, benefit and support of said daughter, Frances, and at her death the property in this bequest mentioned and its increase to be equally divided among her children, share and share alike.

Item eighth; I give and bequeath to my friends, L.A. Weissinger, Geo. T. Johnson & Wm. F. Studwick, in trust for the use, benefit and support of my beloved daughter, Eliza Ann Houze, the remaining third (according to valuation of my negroes not bequeathed to my grandchildren, to be held in Trust by said Trustees for the sole use, benefit, & support, of my said daughter, Eliza, and at her death to be equally divided among her children

Item ninth; It is my will and desire, that my land in Giles County, Tennessee and elsewhere in that State be rented out or sold by my friend, James Patterson & Thomas Martin, of said County of Giles, as they may think most advisable and whom I hereby appoint Trustees for that purpose and

that the proceeds arising from the rent or sale of the aforesaid lands
be paid by the said Trustees, to my Executors, hereinafter named and half
which to be held by them in Trust for the sole use, benefit, & support,
equally to my two daughters, Frances D. Foster, & ElizaAnn House, the
other half to be equally divided among my grandchildren, the whole to be
put at interest by my Executors and by them to be paid either the principal
or interest to my daughters, they may desire the portions going to my
grandchildren to be paid to them as they become of age or marry.

Item. tenth; I do hereby appoint my trusty friends, Leonard A.
Weissinger, George T. Johnson & Wm. F. Studwick, Executors of this my last
will and testament, hereby revoking all other wills by me heretofore made.

In witness whereof, I have hereunto set my hand and seal the day and
date first above written.

DAVID YARBROUGH (Seal)

Signed, sealed , published and
declaired by the said testator,
as for his last will & Testament
in our presence, who at his request in
his presence have subscribed our names
as witness thereto.
John Oswald   )
James D. Brame)
Joel Parish   )

The written Will of David Yarbrough, admitted to probate by the oath
of Joel Parrish. Ordered to be filed & Recorded this 1st day of October
1841

O.C. Eiland, J.C.

The State of Alabama)
Perry County   )   County Court Setting for orphans business the
                             first day of October, A.D. 1841.
Present his Honer Ovid C. Eiland, Judge of said court.
This day came Leonard A. Weissinger, and produced here in open court the
last will & testament of David Yarbrough, deceased and the same being proven
by the oath of Joel Parish, one of the witnesses subscribed thereto, the
same is ordered to be filed and Recorded, and the said Leonard A. Weissinger
George T. Johnson, who was also appointed an Executor's appeared and re-
fused to qualify, and the said Leonard A. Weissinger, Executor, having
entered into bond and security which was approved by the court and ordered
to be filed and recorded.
Ordered by the court that letters of Executorship issue to Leonard
A. Weissinger, on the Estate of David Yarbrough, deceased .

State of Alabama)
Perry County   )

I, Jesse B. Nave, Clerk of the County Court of said County, do hereby
certify that the foregoing is a true copy of the last will and Testament
of David Yarbrough, decd. as filed in this office and a true copy of the
orders proving the same, and the appointment of the Executors to said last
will of said David Yarbrough, decd. In testimony whereof, I have hereunto
set my hand and affixed my seal of said office this 20th day of October,
A.D. 1841.

J.B. Nave, Clerk

JOHN YOUNG

WILL 1837

In the name of God, Amen.
October the 22nd. one thousand eight hundred & thirty seven.

I, John Young of the County of Giles and State of Tennessee, being in good health and calling to mind that it is appointed once fir all men to die, being in my right mind and sences, thanks be to God, for the same, I do make and ordain this my last will and testament, that is to say;

First of all I recommend my soul to God that gave it, my body to the earth to be buried in a decent manner. As to my Estate, my will is all my just debts to be paid, as there has been agreement between me and my beloved wife, Nancy, that her daughter, Frances I. Cravin should have all property that she had before we was married and the part of her father's Estate, all that she had when we were married. Frances I. Cravin, now has gor her part in possession. I will my wife, Nancy Young, the part of the house that she now lives in and cleared land to support her, her life-time. At her death that part of the house and land to belong to Archibald S. Young. I will the part of the land where I now live, to my two sons, Spencer Young, and Archibald Young, to be divided as follows; My son, Spencer, to two part and my son, Archibald S. Young, one part, taking the house where I now live, Spencer Young to have his part in the east end of the tract he geting the best land, Archibald must have the more, the land to be divided agreable to sale without improvements, running from south to north across the tract. I will that my beloved wife, have my two oldest negroes, Hilyard and Pentelope, her lifetime, if she wishes to live in the house I have left her, but if she goes to live with her daughter, Frances I. Cravin, the said Hilyard, Pentelope, to be equally divided with all my children that is living, and I dont wish them parted. I will my beloved wife, one choice horse, and cow & Calf and hogs to supart her. I will Frances Cravin, her mother's bed and furniture at the death of her mother and nothing more, nor her heirs as she has all ready got her mother's Estate, the property left to wife at her death to be equally divided with all my children. I will the land where John Cravin, now lives to William A. Young, my grandson, beginning on the south boundry line and running north with said fenec to the north boundry line, thence west to Buchannans corner, thence south to Buchannan, south east corner, thence east to the beginning. I will my negros to be equally divided with all my children. Spencer Young has received one boy calleded Jeffison, worth five hundred dollars, the others to have one a pease before he gets any more, my daughter Dianna to have her chois of all the women at value. My will is for all my living children to have my negroes, that is to say, Buckner, Rebecca, Dianna, Spencer, and Martha, Archibald, Smith and Nancy. The negroes, Dianna and Rebecca and Martha and Nancy, get to belong to them their lifetime and then to go to the heirs of their body.

I will John W. Fuller, one dollar, I will the children of my daughter, Elizabeth Fuller to have one share to be paid in money to be divided with them, that is to say, Martha Ann, Dolfin, and Ralph, and Archibald, and James Fuller, to have no share in the land. I will the children of my son, Nathaniel Young, one share, but no part of the land as Nathaniel Young has received his part of the land, to be paid in money and to be divided with Caroline, Robert, Nancy, Margaret and Felix Young. I will that tract

of land on Buchannan creek containing fifty acres to be sold, and nine or
ten acres joint entry made by me, and Robert Smith, to belong the land
where I now live, I will my daughter, Dianna, her bed and bedstead and
furniture, and one cow and calf, and all household furniture be sold and
all other property. I will William Young, my Grandson, one share of my
property in money. I do hereby utterly disallow, revoke and disannul
every other former will and testament, legeses by me , anyway before this
time named. Willed this to be my last will and testament. In witness
whereof, I have hereunto set my hand and seal the day & year above written.

                                        JOHN YOUNG (Seal)

Test his
Aaron X Smith, Jurat
        mark
Joseph Smith, Jurat

THOMAS YOUNG

WILL 1841

In the name of God, Amen.

I, Thomas Young, of the State of Tennessee and County of Giles, being of sound mind and memory, and knowing that it is appointed one to die, do make, ordain, this my last will and Testament.

First; It is my will that the tract of land on which I now live containing three hundred and forty acres more or less, be divided as follows; All that part which lies west of Bradshaw's Creek to be divided by straight lines running from the Creek to the west boundary into three equal parts or portions by measure, the middle portion to belong to my son, William Young, his heirs and assigns forever. The other two portions to my sons, Isaac C. Young and Joseph W. Young, their heirs and assigns, forever, and all of said tract of land, east of said creek to be divided in the same manner as that on the west of the same, the middle portion of each side of the creek of said land to be reserved for the use and benefit of my wife, Sarah Young, including the dwelling house, during her natural life, and at the decease to belong to my son, William, his heirs and assigns forever. Each portion so bequeathed, estimated to be worth nine hundred dollars. I bequeath to my wife, Sarah Young, the following property; One gray mare and sorrel yearling colt, Also one wagon, two cows and calves and all the stock of hogs and sheep, with the household & kitchen furniture of every denomination, with the exception of four beds and furniture, which is to be equally divided between my children, Thomas L. Young, William Young, Sarah Ann Young and Martha C. Young. All my farming utensils and such part of the corn and other provisions as may be necessary for the present years allowance, including the stock of bees and also the slaves, Abraham and Hannah, for and during her natural life, and at her death to be sold and the money to be divided equally amongst all those of my children who are intitled to division in the other personal property. But I give my Saint Cloud filly, to my daughter, Sarah Ann Young, and to my daughter, Martha Young, I give my Jackson, horse colt. I wish my blacksmith tools to be sold, the tongs, excepted. Also my clock, shot gun, and wheat fan, and the cattle of every denomination, except one cow & calf, which I gave to each of my children, who may not have received such a gratudy. I also give to my daughter, Martha C. Young, twenty five dollars in money to purchase a saddle for her sole use and benefit, and whereas my son, John C. Young, has received fifty dollars, in a horse, more than the rest of my children, I desire that sum to be deducted out of what is coming to him. I desire that the following slaves, towot; Bonds, Mima, Henry, Cynthia, Richard, Adam, Emmily, America, Gilbert, and Price, be sold with all other property and stock, not heretofore reserved, to be sold by my Executors immediately after my decease, ot at such other time as they may deem proper and expedient, and the proceeds to be equally divided between my children, Mary Holly, John C. Young, Thomas L. Young, Dorothy Harwell, Sarah Ann Young, & Martha C. Young, in such manner that each of them may receive a sum equal to nine hundred dollars, and if any more should remain after making such division that the residue, after paying all my just debts be equally divided between all of my children; share and share, alike. I hereby nominate my sons, Thomas L. and William Young, my Executors, to this my last will and testament, Signed, sealed and declaired in presence of us, to be his last will and testament, 28th April, A.D. 1841.

THOMAS X YOUNG (Seal)

Attest. Obediah Pinson, Jurat
William Noxbey, Jurat
Ellis Suttle, Jurat

THOMAS L. YOUNG

WILL 1843

I, Thomas L. Young, do make and publish this my last will and Testament, hereby revoking and making void, all other wills by me at any time made.

First; I direct that my funeral expenses and all my debts be paid as soon after my death as possible, out of any moneys that I may die possessed of, or may first come into the hands of my Executor.

Secondly: I bequeath to my wife, Laticia C. Young, one negro woman named, Caroline, one negro boy named Henry, of Giles County, a negro boy named, Adam, this boy, Adam is to be hired out four years, and half of the hire to be given to my sister, Martha, to pay her tuition, the other half to my wife, Laticia.

Fifthly: I do bequeath to my wife, seven hundred dollars, more or less in notes that I hold in my hands.

Sixly: I do bequeath to my beloved wife, Laticia, my Charly horse, and carriage, and Harness,

Seventhly: I do bequeath a certain bay mare and colt, to Thomas T. Young, the son of my brother, Joseph Young, and that the mare and colt be sold when thought the best and the money be put on interest, until it can be approrpiated to pay his tuition by the executor of this will.

Eighthly and lastly: I do bequeath to my beloved wife, Laticia, all my household and kitchen furniture, and lastly I do nominate and appoint John C. Young, my Executor. In witness whereof, I do to this my last will set my hand and seal this 20th of June, 1843, Signed, sealed and published, in our presence and we have subscribed our names hereto in presence of testators this the 20th. of June 1843.

John H. Birdsong,

Ira B. Brown, Jurat

THOS. L. YOUNG (Seal)